REMEMBERING BELLOC

Other Titles of Interest from St. Augustine's Press

James V. Schall, *The Regensburg Lecture*

James V. Schall, *The Modern Age*

James V. Schall, *Sum Total of Human Happiness*

James V. Schall, *The Classical Moment: Selected Essays on Knowledge and Its Pleasures*

Marc D. Guerra, ed., *Jerusalem, Athens, and Rome: Essays in Honor of James V. Schall, S.J.*

Robert Royal, ed., *The Catholic Thing: Five Years of a Singular Website*

Rémi Brague, *Eccentric Culture*

Rémi Brague, *On the God of the Christians (and on one or two others)*

C.S. Lewis & St. Giovanni Calabria, *The Latin Letters of C.S. Lewis*

Josef Pieper, *Happiness and Contemplation*

Josef Pieper, *The Christian Idea of Man*

Josef Pieper, *The Platonic Myths*

George William Rutler, *Principalities and Powers: Spiritual Combat 1942–1943*

H.S. Gerdil, *The Anti-Emile: Reglections on the Theory and Practice of Education against the Principles of Rousseau*

Gerhart Niemeyer, *The Loss and Recovery of Truth*

Roger Kimball, *The Fortunes of Permanence*

Pope Pius VI, *The French Revolution Confronts Pius VI* (in 2 vols.)

Karol Wojtyła [John Paul II], *Man in the Field of Responsibility*

Gabriel Marcel, *Man against Mass Society*

Gabriel Marcel, *The Mystery of Being* (in 2 vols.)

Peter Augustine Lawler, *Homeless and at Home in America: Evidence for the Dignity of the Human Soul in Our Time and Place*

Roger Scruton, *An Intelligent Person's Guide to Modern Culture*

Peter Kreeft, *Summa Philosophica*

Edward Feser, *Last Superstition: A Refutation of the New Atheism*

Jacques Maritain, *Natural Law: Reflections on Theory and Practice*

REMEMBERING BELLOC

James V. Schall, S.J.

Foreword by Rev. C.J. McCloskey III

ST. AUGUSTINE'S PRESS
South Bend, Indiana

Manufactured in the United States of America

1 2 3 4 5 6   19 18 17 16 15 14 13

Library of Congress Cataloging in Publication Data
Schall, James V.
Remembering Belloc / James V. Schall; foreword by C.J. McCloskey
III.
p. cm.
Includes bibliographical references.
ISBN 978-1-58731-703-3 (hardcover: alk. paper)
1. Belloc, Hilaire, 1870–1953 – Criticism and interpretation.
2. Belloc, Hilaire, 1870–1953 – Political and social views.
3. Belloc, Hilaire, 1870–1953. I. Title.
PR6003.E45Z84 2013
828'.91209 – dc23   2012039814

∞ The paper used in this publication meets the minimum requirements of the American National Standard for Information Sciences Permanence of Paper for Printed Materials, ANSI Z39.481984.

St. Augustine's Press
www.staugustine.net

"And, indeed, it is very ridiculous the way in which men try to withstand this influence of their enemy, Time. They had far better accept the condition of mortality and remember a truth which was plainly painted in large black letters upon a large white placard in Eden, which was restated by Dante, and then repeated by Malherbe, that our only peace lies in the doing of God's will; which includes going to pieces in the fifties, or sixties, or seventies, like an old disreputable, sodden, broken-down hulk too long adventured upon the sea."

—Belloc, *The Cruise of the Nona*
(Boston: Houghton Mifflin, 1925), 186–87.

"I read somewhere that negative things can not impress the mind; that mere absence, a mere void, leaves no stamp upon the memory. I may have thought so before I first stood (so many years ago!) upon the lift of the Byrsa, on the slight slope of what had been the citadel of so famous a state. But since that date I have always known that the death of things can be impressive as the death of men."

—Belloc, "The Hill of Carthage," *Towns of Destiny*
(New York: McBride, MCMXXVII), 122.

"I have sometimes wondered whether it might not be possible to have guide books written for the great routes of modern travel—I mean of modern pleasure-travel—which should make the whole road a piece of history; for history enlarges everything one sees, and gives a fullness to flat experience, so that one lives more than one's own life in contemplating it, and so that new landscapes are not only new for a moment, but subject to centuries of varieties in one's mind."

—Belloc, "On the History of Travel," *Selected Essays*
(London: Methuen, 1948), 30.

"If a man tells you it 'stands to reason' that a just God could not allow men to lose their souls, he suffers from the Scepticism of the Stupid. The Scepticism proceeding from intelligence is of an exactly opposite nature. Intelligence may be measured by the capacity of separating categories. . . . The man who distinguished between the two meanings of a word often used in two senses is more intelligent than the man who does not."

—Belloc, "The Approach to the Sceptic," *Essays of a Catholic*
(London: Sheed & Ward, MCMXXXI), 52–53.

"Friends of mine, friends all, and you also, publishers, colonials and critics, do you know that particular experience for which I am trying to find words? Do you know that glamour in the mind which arises and transforms our thought when we see the things that the men who made us saw—the things of a long time ago, the origins? I think everybody knows that glamour, but very few people know where to find it."

—Belloc, "The Channel," *Hills and the Sea*
(Marlboro, Vt.:The Marlboro Press, 1906), 138.

"Look you, good people all, in your little passage through the daylight, get to see as many hills and buildings and rivers, fields, books, men, horses, ships, and precious stones as you can possibly manage to do. Or else stay in one village and marry in it and die there. For one of these two fates is the best fate for every man. Either to be what I have been, a wanderer with all the bitterness of it, or to stay at home and hear in one's garden the voice of God."

—Belloc, "The Death of Wandering Peter," *Selected Essays*
(Penguin, 1958), 75.

Table of Contents

Acknowledgments

The author would like to thank the Director of the American Chesterton Society, Mr. Dale Ahlquist, for permission to use essays on Belloc that were originally in *Generally Speaking*, the early newsletter of the American Chesterton Society, and in *Gilbert Magazine*.

Though these essays have been somewhat edited for this volume the following chapters originally appeared from 1996–97, in *Generally Speaking:* Chapters 2, 5, 7, 9, 11, 12, 13, 14, 15, and 22.

The author also wishes to thank the editors of *Crisis Magazine, The Fellowship of Catholic Scholars Quarterly, Catholic Dossier, Excelsis, Saint Austin Review, ISI Books, The London Catholic Truth Society,* and St. Benedict's Press for permission to use materials published in their books and journals.

—Preface, *Crisis*, June 2003; Chapter 23, *Crisis*, November 1994

Foreword

It is an honor for me as a great admirer of both Father James Schall, S.J. and Hilaire Belloc to introduce this book to you the reader. Only two years ago Fr. Schall kindly wrote the introduction to *The Essential Belloc* (Saint Benedict Press), a book that I co-edited with Brian Robertson and Scott Bloch.

In a certain sense the two books are joined at the hip, since Fr. Schall's *Remembering Belloc* serves as the hermeneutic for *The Essential Belloc,* which serves up quotes that are explained by Fr. Schall's brilliant insights into the person and writings of Belloc.

Fr. Schall himself, besides being a long-time professor at Georgetown University in Washington, D.C., is a prolific writer of over thirty books and hundreds of book reviews, essays, and occasional columns. As a native Washingtonian who directed the Catholic Information Center in D.C for five years, I can attest to the powerful influence that Fr. Schall continues to exert over both undergraduate and graduate students, many of whom have converted to the Catholic faith under his influence (not unlike Belloc's influence on the immortal G. K. Chesterton, another of Fr. Schall's favorite authors and the subject of some of his previous writing). In future decades people may be elucidating the works and thinking of Fr. Schall in doctoral dissertations and books similar to the one I am introducing.

I believe it was Evelyn Waugh who said that Belloc was the best prose stylist of the twentieth century—high praise, even though or perhaps because Belloc said something similar about P. G. Wodehouse.

Now, Belloc was not as funny as Wodehouse (biting wit and satire being the type of humor Belloc most commonly committed to writing), but then again, perhaps not until Dr. Seuss did any man make more children laugh than Belloc did with his *Cautionary Tales for Children* and his *The Bad Child's Book of Beasts.*

Schall's title *Remembering Belloc* is significant, as it applies to the author's many decades of reading and rediscovering a man whose life from at least his student years at Oxford was dedicated to "remembering" what was being forgotten—that is, the history and heritage of the"West" that has now largely disappeared.

Another word for the West is "Christendom." It is the culture that grew from the rich soil of the classical world following God's redemptive intervention in sending his son to redeem us. Jesus then left us an institution to guide us through this life and into heaven. This universal institution, which we call the Catholic Church, Belloc often referred to as "the Thing" to stress that it is a reality and not merely an idea (Chesterton used the term to christen a collection of his essays on the Church).

Belloc consecrated himself defender, historian, and troubadour of the Church—and all without footnotes, since he had nothing to prove. He had certainly read all the relevant books, but he had gone far beyond the standard historian—he had sailed, walked, and scaled virtually all of Europe in numerous trips to see with his own eyes what other historians only wrote about. He listened to the music, viewed the art (his French grandfather being a fine artist), visited the cathedrals, and walked the battlefields of generals from Hannibal to Marshal Foch. He ate the cheese and drank the fine red wine of Christian Europe and foresaw almost exactly what we are now living through, the revival of Islam and the emergence of "The Servile State."

As a child, Belloc was taught by a future saint, the greatest Catholic theologian of the nineteenth century, Blessed John Henry Newman (who also was a significant historian and indeed prophet).

Both teacher and student ultimately saw liberalism as the devolvement of Christendom and the West, a descent inevitable unless it could be successfully combated by Catholic men and women living this life looking forward to the next. Whether we are entering into a new age of evangelization, as Blessed John Paul the Great thought, or perhaps shrinking into "a creative minority" as Pope Benedict XVI posits, only future historians will tell.

In the meantime, enjoy this delightful introduction to Hilaire Belloc by his most knowledgeable disciple, Fr. James Schall of Georgetown. Happily, dozens of Belloc's books are still in print for your further reading pleasure once you've worked up an appetite from reading Fr. Schall's book. Together they are just the tonic to rouse readers to the Crusading zeal of Belloc himself to defend the West.

Fr. C. J. McCloskey III is a Church Historian and Research Fellow at the Faith and Reason Institute in Washington, DC.

Preface

Hilaire Belloc died on Sunday, July 12, 1953. He was, as I will often remind the reader, simply the best essayist in our language. If someone asks me what is Belloc's greatest essay, I have to say, honestly, "the last one I read." I love his essay on the English city of "Lynn" in *Hills and the Sea*. His essay on "Jane Austen" (*Selected Essays*, Penguin) has more to say about men and women than we can find in a million dull books on the topic. "The End of Chateaubriand," in *Miniatures of French History,* always recalls to me my chance reading, in the Novitiate at Los Gatos, of an old copy of Chateaubriand's *The Genius of Christianity*, a book that enchanted me. It was in this Belloc essay that I read, "It was November—*the most lonely month of the year"* (277). Indeed, I wrote a "Sense and Nonsense" column on it (November, 1994) that will be included here (Chapter 23).

Ever since 9/11 and the wars with Muslim terrorists, Belloc's shadow continually rises over our generation. He understood what our social sciences prevent us from understanding, the power of spiritual forces, for good or ill. To read his discussion of Islam in his *Great Heresies*, written in 1938, is like reading contemporary history. In a way, it is reading contemporary history. If we hesitate to understand the importance of battles in the history of man, we would do well to read *The Crusades,* in which he tells us what an enormous difference military battles, both those lost and those won, makes.

A phrase in his *Life of Danton* reads: "By the irony of whatever rules and laughs at men" (364). Belloc, of course was a Catholic, a "born Catholic," as he said of himself. It is a good thing, he remarked in *The Path to Rome* (1901), "never to have to return to the faith," though he had youthful doubts. Yet, we find a certain existential sad-

1

ness in Belloc. His was a life of disappointment and song, of conversation and brooding silence. I often touch on this sadness.

"Why should the less gracious part of a pilgrimage be specifically remembered?" Belloc asked himself in *The Path to Rome*. "In life we remember joy best—that is what makes us sad by contrast" (185). In life, we remember joy best. Joy is not unacquainted with its opposite. Indeed, we seem to need sadness to understand joy, as least most of us do. Even though we belong to the religion of the Cross, or perhaps, because we belong to it, joy is higher in rank than sadness.

Belloc's father was French, his mother English, his wife an American from Napa, California. He lost one son in World War I and another in World War II. He wrote on every subject known to man and God and, at least till he thought them up, on a few things that were known to neither!

To me, amidst the obvious confusion at the heart of Catholicism today, his words from his classic walk, *The Path to Rome*, are of considerable consolation. As we grow older, he wrote, we worry about the "human machinery of a perfect and superhuman revelation" (102). We do indeed.

No one is more nostalgic than Belloc. In an essay, "The Portrait of a Child" (*Selected Essays*, Penguin), he asks: "Do you know that that which smells most strongly in this life of immortality, and which a poet has called 'the ultimate outpost of eternity,' is insecure and perishes?" No, we did not know that! Whatever was the man talking about? The "strong smell in this life of immortality?" What "outpost of eternity?"

"I mean," Belloc explains, "the passionate affection of early youth. If that does not remain, what then do you think can remain?" "Yes, what does remain?" we wonder. Belloc levels with us, we who perhaps have forgotten the "passionate affection of early youth." "I tell you that nothing which you take to be permanent round about you when you are very young is more than the symbol or clothes of permanence." Belloc speaks of the holiness, sanctity of lives that we catch in childhood portraits—he speaks of what is "true of all that little passage of ours through the daylight."

No book is quite like *The Four Men*. This is Belloc's walk in his own land in 1902. This book too is simply an enchantment. My copy, alas, is falling apart, though fortunately I have a second one. In this book, Belloc himself appears as "Myself," but also as a sailor, a poet, and an old man, all of which he was in his day. "We have come to the term and boundary of this short passage of ours, and of our brief companionship. . . ." These words refer not only to a walk in Sussex, his home county, but to our lives themselves, the "little passage of ours through the daylight."

Over the years, I have given lectures and written essays, often brief, on Belloc. What I hoped to do someday is to collect them together, as "my Belloc." I will not much go into the many controversies and issues of Belloc's life, his time in Parliament, his relation to Oxford, his family, style and approach to history, politics, the faith in Europe, the history of England, and philosophy.

What I want to show is how Belloc can reach our souls. Thus, I have called these essays, "Remembering Belloc." I have left them pretty much as I wrote them, so common themes will often reappear. I think it best to let them be heard again rather than edit them out. They are written in different times and occasions, but each is occasioned by what Belloc saw and thought.

For a while, I did a series for a newsletter called *Generally Speaking* called "Schall on Belloc." Many of these essays are found here. I have a book called *Schall on Chesterton*, and a long series of essays in *Gilbert Magazine* by the same title. Obviously, I have great admiration for both of these good men who were themselves friends and often rightly thought of together.

What I want of this book is a true "remembering," that is, a bringing to life the wonder another man was able to create in one's soul by his descriptions and accounts of what he saw and what he thought. One of Belloc's greatest comments is in *The Four Men* in which he said that the only way we can keep a place is by remembering it. As I like to say, "to remember is to keep." And Belloc is worthy of being kept.

In this book, most chapters will be relatively short. The first chapter in each part will be longer, but never too long, I hope. Thus, each of the six parts will begin with a longer essay and end with four shorter ones. Each part will begin with a citation from Belloc.

An earlier book of mine was entitled, *Idylls and Rambles: Shorter*

Christian Essays.[1] In large part the shorter essays in this book arise directly from reading Belloc. The longer ones from reflecting on him and what he taught us. The short essay is something I have always been fond of. I find that often its conciseness makes both better reading and better thinking. But I love the essay in general. It is not a "thesis" yet often can do in the modern world what the thesis form cannot, that is, arouse our interest and attention when we are not expecting it.

Belloc himself was a gifted writer of almost every form of literature. He wrote war books, history books, apologetic books, political books, lyrical essays, poetry, novels, and nostalgic recollections. I have, I hope, touched here on the heart of Belloc. I "remember" Belloc not just because he is worth remembering to generations not likely to know of him, but because he lightens the mind and soul of man about the permanent things in this world, a world, as Belloc was always fully aware, that was in fact passing before his very eyes.

If we remember Belloc, we will remember much of which we not only need to know, but of what we are delighted and charmed in knowing. There is something almost mystical about Belloc, what he saw, where he saw it, how it brought him to ultimate things. Some of this soul-stirring mood, I hope, is caught in these essays. It is not enough, I think, that Belloc wrote them. We too must read. We too have souls that are touched when one of our kind sees the permanence and enduring things midst the passingness of our lives about which we are constantly aware.

Part 1

"Do you not notice how the intimate mind of Europe is reflected in cheese? For in the centre of Europe, and where Europe is most active, I mean in Britain and in Gaul and in northern Italy, and in the valley of the Rhine—nay, to some extent in Spain (in her Pyrenean valleys at least)—there flourishes a vast burgeoning of cheese, infinite in variety, one in goodness. But as Empire fades away under the African wound which Spain suffered or the Eastern barbarians of the Elbe, what happens to cheese? It becomes very flat and similar. You can quote six cheeses perhaps which the public power of Christendom has founded outside the limits of its ancient Empire—but not more than six. I will quote you 253 between the Ebro and the Grampians, between Brindisi and the Irish Channel. *I do not write vainly. It is a profound thing.*"

—Hilaire Belloc, "On Cheeses," *Selected Writings*, Penguin.

Chapter 1

"ON THE CHARACTER
OF ENDURING THINGS"

"And on this account, Sussex, does a man love an old house,
which was his father's, and on this account does a man come
to love with all his heart, that part of earth which nourished
his boyhood. For it does not change, or if it changes, it
changes very little, and he finds in it *the character of enduring things*."

—Belloc, The Four Men, Preface.[1]

I.

This book will begin by remembering two walks of Belloc. The man
was a walker. The books recall his two walks and set the stage for the
memory of permanent things that Belloc wanted to be ours. They are
journeys we all should take. We do so by reading him and filling our
souls with places we never forget. Because someone else writes, we can
"see" many things we cannot visit in our own time.

The Path to Rome recounted the walk that Belloc took by himself
from his old French army post in Toul to fulfill his vow to reach High
Mass at St. Peter's in Rome on the Feast of Sts. Peter and Paul, the
twenty-ninth of June. This walk took place in 1901.[2] We will return to
it later and often mention it. The following year, 1902, Belloc records a
second equally "wonder-full" walk that he took in his home county of
Sussex in England. The termination of both these walks, one suspects,
was the same, albeit one ending at St. Peter's, the other at his own
home. On second thought the first walk did not exactly finish with
Mass at St. Peter's. As he tells us, Belloc arrived when Mass was just

ending. A priest told him in Latin that the next one would begin in twenty minutes. So he added twenty minutes to his pilgrimage and thus delightfully to his book.

During this extra time, Belloc, crossing St. Peter's Square, with no little amused irony, passed by an "Egyptian obelisk which the great Augustus had nobly dedicated to the Sun." "The Reader" then wanted to know, after all this wandering about Europe, whether he planned to say anything of Rome itself? "Nothing, dear Lector," Belloc retorted. Instead, while waiting, he went into a café down a long narrow street, where he "called for bread, coffee, and brandy." In the remaining few moments, he wrote doggerel verses summing up his now completed "Path" to Rome—"Drinking when I had a mind to, / Singing when I felt inclined to; / Nor ever turned my face to home / Till I had slaked my heart at Rome."

The Four Men also ends with verse: "When friend and fire and home are lost / And even children drawn away— / The passer-by shall hear me still, / A boy that sings on Duncton Hill." Belloc concludes the second walk simply, "full of these thoughts and greatly relieved by their metrical expression, I went, through the gathering darkness, southward across the Downs to my home."" For Belloc, the kinship between home and Rome was not accidental.

The second walk lasts from the twenty-ninth of October to the second day of November, 1902. Included, in other words, with all their symbolisms, are All Hallows' Eve, All Hallows' Day, and All Souls' Day—the "Day of the Dead," as Belloc named it. These solemn days recall the human condition—we live, we sin, we repent, or perhaps we don't. From the beginning, what we are destined for, even if we do not reach it, is glory. But, as Belloc is aware, some there are, Pelagians all, who claim that they need no grace to attain such glory and are proudly confident that they can save themselves.

Later, outside the Crabtree Inn on the 31st of October, the four men, whom we shall soon meet, stop for beer and cheese. The Sailor decides to sing "in a very full and decisive manner" (48). The song that he chooses is marvelously entitled, "Song of the Pelagian Heresy for the Strengthening of Men's Backs and the very Robust Out-thrusting of Doubtful Doctrine and the Uncertain Intellectual." No song-title is better suited to our time of doubtful doctrines and uncertain intellectuals who seek to accomplish everything, even their own salvation, for and by themselves.

Belloc gives the musical notes and the words of this little Pelagian tune. The words are remarkable: "Pelagius lived in Kardanoel, / And taught a doctrine there, / How whether you went to Heaven or Hell, / It was your own affair. / How, whether you found eternal joy / Or sank forever to burn, / It had nothing to do with the Church, my boy, / But was your own concern." One of the fellow walkers called this doctrine "blasphemous," but the Sailor maintained it was "orthodox," which it wasn't without the awareness of grace.

Belloc proceeded to sing the final "semi-chorus," as it is called: "Oh, he didn't believe / In Adam and Eve, / He put no faith therein! / His doubts began / With the fall of man, / And he laughed at original sin." The verses go on to recount the whole history of such heresy in song—no doubt the only way it should be studied. All utopias begin, I suspect, by this "laughing at original sin." They all end as a result by making things worse by "having nothing to do with the Church."

II.

Belloc likewise records the tradition, not to be found specifically in Genesis, to be sure, that the Garden of Eden was originally found in his home county. On finishing this book, we can well believe it. He gives the following account of this local lore:

> When Adam was out (with the help of Eve) to name all the places of the earth (and that is why he had to live so long), he desired to distinguish Sussex, late his happy seat, by some special mark which would pick it out from all the other places of the earth, its inferiors and vassals. So that when Paradise might be regained and the hopeless generation of men permitted to pass the Flaming Sword at Shiremark Mill, and to see once more the four rivers, Arun and Adur, and Cuckmere and Ouse, they might know their native place again and mark it for Paradise (43).

The method Adam used to accomplish this special marking of Paradise that is Sussex was that, in this county alone, everything would be called

9

by its opposite geographical name. Down would be called Up, and North would be called South. Moreover, "no one in the County should pronounce 'th,' 'ph,' or 'sh,' but always 'h' separately, under pain of damnation." For Belloc not only were Rome and home identified, but both commenced in that Paradise originally located in the county of Sussex, Belloc's own county.

As I try to read T. S. Eliot's poem "Ash Wednesday" every Ash Wednesday, so I endeavor to reread every year Belloc's *Four Men* during these five "All Hallows" days. Belloc is right; enduring things are found here in this book, including a certain sadness that always seems to be about Belloc, in spite of his amazing jollity. Belloc, almost as much as Plato, is poignantly aware of the passingness of life and the need to attach what happens in time to more eternal things.

The Preface of *The Four Men* begins, "My county, it has been proved in the life of every man that though his loves are human, and therefore changeable, yet in proportion as he attaches them to things unchangeable, so they mature and broaden. On this account, Dear Sussex, are those women chiefly dear to men who, as the seasons pass, do but continue to be more and more themselves, attain balance, and abandon or forget vicissitude." Belloc's enduring things include the things he knew, the ones he loved, particularly the women.

The Four Men describes a walk through Sussex. The book includes maps, songs, sketches, and drawings. It is a perfect multi-media book and would make a wonderful film but only by a director wise enough not to change a word of the text. The sketches of the bridges, the stone buildings, the valleys are especially fine. The "four" men are each Belloc himself. They are called respectively, "Myself," "Grizzlebeard," "the Poet," and "the Sailor."

In his complete life, Belloc, of course, was each of these men. He himself had sailed the seas, we remember the cruise of the Nona, written verses, and would grow old. He was a man who did not forget what he saw or knew. He loved companionship, but he also realized that it did not remain, however important it was while it lasted. "Myself" remarks to Grizzlebeard, after they agree to walk together, "for all companionship is good, but chance companionship is best of all. . . ." (5). We shall return to the end of companionship when the four cease to walk together.

The walk began on October 29, 1902, at an Inn, called the "George," at Robertsbridge. Alone, "Myself" sat drinking a glass of port. "Multitude of thoughts" came into his head but most importantly "the vision of the woods of home and of another place—the place where the (river) Arun rises." He talks to himself. He mocks himself that the purpose of his business far away seems to be only "to make money," the result of which he will return to spend more than he earns. What about ultimate things? He chides himself, "all the while your life runs past you like a river, and the things that are of moment to men you do not heed at all." The things that "are of moment to men" are indeed usually ignored until Belloc decides to walk in Sussex.

This is what *The Four Men* is about, the things that we should heed lest they run past us like a river. Or as he says to himself, "what you are doing is not worth while, and nothing is worth while on this unhappy earth except the fulfillment of a man's desire." It is at this point in his solitary broodings that "Myself" first meets Grizzlebeard, a man "full of travel and of sadness." They also meet the Sailor. They agree to walk together to the end of Sussex. "This older man and I have inclined ourselves to walk westward with no plan, until we come to the better parts of the county, that is, to Arun and to the land I know," Myself explains to the Sailor.

As the walk begins, the three finally run into the fourth companion, a youthful Poet. "His eyes were arched and large as though in a perpetual surprise, and they were of a warm grey colour. They did not seem to see the things before them, but other things beyond; and while the rest of his expression changed a little to greet us, his eyes did not change. Moreover, they seemed continually sad." Grizzlebeard, "as though he was his father," tells the Poet that these three are good men. He will enjoy the walk. "Only come westward with us and be our companion until we go to the place where the sun goes down, and discover what makes it so glorious" (16). Who could resist such a destination, where the Sun goes down, to discover "what makes it so glorious?"

As they continue their walk through Sussex, each recounts things that he knew of the area. They all know the geography and lore of the place. The first story has to do with St. Dunstan. This is a wild narrative of how St. Dunstan tricked the Devil and thus caused a great moat to be built in the land. Belloc includes some wise demonology, reminis-cent of the lies that this same tainted gentleman told our mother Eve in the Sussex Paradise: "And indeed this is the Devil's way, always to pre-tend that he is the master, though he very well knows in his black heart that he is nothing of the kind" (19).

III.

One of the remarkable things about Belloc is the place that food plays in his life, vivid and concrete reminders of our incarnational existence. He would certainly have disdained and mocked modern dietary admo-nitions about cholesterol and calories. My favorite Belloc meal is the following. The last light of the day had disappeared. "The air was pure and cold, as befitted All-Hallows. . . ." (146). The four men reached the edge of the Downs headed for the Hampshire border. Mist was on the Rother. They came to an old inn.

Sounds of singing from inside the inn greeted them. The men singing seemed to be farmers on a sales day. The bar of the inn was ele-gant. Some fifteen men were inside harmonizing and drinking. The four men were tired and the other party would last long. The four were thus served at another table. What did they eat after their long day's march? The meal consisted

> of such excellence in the way of eggs and bacon, as we had none of us until that moment thought possible upon this side of the grave. The cheese also . . . was put before us, and the new cottage loaves, so that this feast, unlike any other feast that yet was since the beginning of the world, exactly answered all that the heart had expected of it, and we were contented and were filled (147).

I would hesitate to count the caloric intake here, but such a feast, "this side of the grave," in its description surely fulfills what Leon Kass, in his great book, called *The Hungry Soul Eating and the Perfection of Our Nature*.[3]

After this feast, it was time for a pipe. Each called for his own drink. "Myself" had "black currant port." Grizzlebeard chose brandy. The Sailor bought the Poet beer, while the Sailor sipped claret. They then join the group of farmers. They sing together the rousing "Golier."

This scene recalls that wonderful institution the inn. The Sailor, who has seen the world, remarks, "there is not upon this earth so good a thing as an inn; but even among good things there must be hierarchy" (62). The best inn in the world, we are told, was the Inn at Bramber; now forgotten, it will not return. The great inns are listed. Their very names charm us and take us out of ourselves: the Star of Yarmouth, the Dolphin at Southampton, the Bridge Inn of Amberley, the White Hart of Storrington, the Spread Eagle of Midhurst, "that oldest and most revered of all the prime inns of this world," the White Hart of Steyning, the White Horse of Storrington, and the Swan of Pentworth.

Our business sees that these "were only mortal inns, human inns, full of a common and reasonable good; but round the Inn at Bramber, my companions, there hangs a very different air" (63). This is the inn of memory, so perfect that it cannot be visited again. "And what purpose would it serve to shock once more that craving of the soul for certitude and for repose?" Indeed, what purpose would it serve?

The conversation along the paths of Sussex is of battles and loves, of earthy things like fires and breakfast and ale. The best of ales is named in the Sailor's famous All Hallows' Day song: "May all good fellows that here agree / Drink Audit Ale in heaven with me, / And may all my enemies go to hell! / Noël! Noël! Noël! Noël!" (126). But midst this levity, we find an amazing profundity to their conversation.

The mystery of how we stand to one another in the highest things comes back again and again. "Everything else that there is in the action of the mind save loving," Grizzlebeard points out, "is of its nature a growth: it goes through its phases of seed, of miraculous sprouting, of maturity, of somnolescence, and of decline. But with loving it is not so; for the comprehension by one soul of another is something borrowed from whatever lies outside time: it is not under the confines of time. Then if it passes, it is past—it never grows again: and we lose it as men lose a diamond, or as men lose their honour" (27). "Myself" objects that loss of honor is worse than loss of friends' love.

Grizzlebeard did not think so. Honor is outside of us. We do not give it to ourselves. "Not so men who lose the affection of a creature's eyes. Therein for them, I mean in death, is no solution." What concerns Grizzlebeard is the mystery of the "passing of affection." Love is not under the confines of time, neither in its coming nor in its going.

Belloc is never too far from warning us of the machinations of the academic and intellectual mind. "Myself" at one point remarks that "the Poet was now thoroughly annoyed, not being so companionable a man (by reason of his trade) as he might be. For men become companionable by working with their bodies and not with their weary noddles, and the spinning out of stuff from oneself is an inhuman thing" (123). We only know ourselves when we first know what is not ourselves. Much of modernity is concerned with "spinning out stuff from oneself."

On the final day, the four men arise early to end their chance companionship. They know they will never meet again. Grizzlebeard touchingly sums up their experience:

> There is nothing at all that remains: nor any house, nor any castle, however strong, nor any love, however tender and sound, nor any comradeship among men however hardy. Nothing remains but the things of which I will not speak, because we have spoken enough of them already during these four days. But I who am old will give you advice, which is this—to consider chiefly from now onward those permanent things which are, as it were, the shores of this age and the harbours of our glittering and pleasant but dangerous and wholly changeful sea (157–58).

Grizzlebeard speaks here of death. The four then pause "for about the time which a man can say good-bye with reverence." They go their own ways. "Myself" watches them depart "straining my sad eyes." He then returns to the Downs and his home.

Chapter 2

ON ENDURANCE AND FORTITUDE

In an essay, "On Fortitude," in the Penguin edition of his *Selected Essays,* Belloc tells of the unusual cathedral of Périgueux, its massive, sheer stones.[1] But it was not the Cathedral itself that he wrote of here. It was something that he recalled years later. He had once seen something in the Cathedral that struck him. He still remembers his being moved by what he saw, something that seems so incidental, so insignificant in itself, that he is surprised to remember it. He wondered a bit about how we could suddenly find ourselves meditating on some odd incident of our life, something that apparently made no visible difference, yet it kept coming back.

Indeed, Belloc took some time to reflect on how chance things can often change our lives. It is a beautiful passage:

> It has been remarked by men from the beginning of time that chance connections may determine thought: a chance tune heard in unexpected surroundings, a chance sentence not addressed perhaps to oneself and having no connection with the circumstances around, the chance sight of an unexpected building appearing round the corner of a road, the chance glance of an eye that will never meet our eyes again—any one of these things may establish a whole train of contemplation which takes root and inhabits the mind forever.

We have no doubt that each of these items—the tune, the sentence, the building, the glance—were incidents in Belloc's life, things he never quite forgot.

The chance event that remained to inhabit his mind "forever," of which he writes here, took place in the very massive and strangely cupola-ed, almost Byzantine or Moorish Cathedral in this city in south-western France, in the Department of Périgord. On the right side of the northern transept of this Cathedral—he does not explain how he happened to be there—there was a bare, gigantic arch with a mosaic of an Elephant under which was found the word "Fortitude." The Elephant was immense too, like the stones in the Cathedral. The Elephant, like the huge stones, seemed the perfect symbol of this virtue.

Fortitude (bravery) is found there enshrined in a Christian Church because "it is one of the great virtues." What does fortitude imply? It implies "endurance: that character that we need the most in the dark business of life." Belloc reminds us that sometimes, often perhaps, the "the business of life" is "dark," unpleasant, dire. Terrible things sometimes have to be faced, have to be borne with.

Several words cluster about this notion of fortitude—which itself means patient courage, not just courage, but patient courage. Courage itself indicates the habit by which we rule our fears and pains so that we can reach our end. This is Aristotle and Aquinas. Courage is necessarily at the basis of all the other virtues because it is directed to life itself, to existence and its preservation. But it has the connotation of a life standing for something. Courage is the opposite of cowardice. The courageous man endures; the coward gives up. If the courageous man dies, the principle for which he dies remains intact. If he stays alive no matter what, yielding to every threat, he stands only for himself, for an existence that means nothing but itself.

Bravery adds to courage a certain daring, a boldness in the face of a threat to life or honor. Valor means the continuous presence of bravery, the lofty quality of being brave not just once but over time in the face of many hardships and dangers. But, as St. Thomas said, the primary act of courage is not to attack but to endure, even to suffer. This does not mean that courage is a kind of silly pacifism. It means the courage of the martyr, as Josef Pieper pointed out, the one who endures what can no longer be avoided, endures in what he affirms.

Fortitude, Belloc remarked, must be not just endurance but "creative endurance." It involves some memory of a better time and some hope of its return. Belloc, we know, was a military man in his youth. He loved to follow the lines of battle, to reflect on the course of war in the very place of combat. He understood that with no fortitude, there would be no civilization. "The thing, Fortitude, is the opposite of aggressive, flamboyant courage, yet it is the greater of the two, though often it lacks action."

Fortitude wears armor and holds a sword, but it "stands ready rather than thrusts itself forward." The phrase "lacks action" said of fortitude needs reflection. Belloc's passage is at first sight a version of "if you want peace, prepare for war." It is also contains a sense of caution, a restraint on any untoward eagerness to "thrust forward." It contains the experience of mankind. If it uses the sword, it does so reluctantly, knowing what is at stake. Suffering evil rather than doing it, as Joseph Pieper has said, is the greatest act of fortitude.[2]

Belloc then spent a page in recounting the effects of this enduring fortitude during the dark and middle ages, when it looked like all was lost for Christendom. In the ninth and tenth centuries, with enemies on its south, east, and north, Europe should not have survived. But it did largely because of the Elephant of Périgueux, because of Fortitude. "The West rose up again in glory, having been saved by Fortitude."

Today, it seems almost eccentric to attribute anything to a virtue, to a virtue whose act is to rule our fears and our pains. Belloc did not write of arms or of strategy; he wrote of a virtue. "Fortitude does not envisage new things, rather does it tenaciously preserve things known and tried." Thus, fortitude implies that there are things worth preserving. Without this latter sense, there can be no proper fortitude, no endurance, no resistance.

Fortitude for its own sake is in fact a vice. Fortitude is for a reason, for a purpose, for the highest reason and purpose of all, the reason of why we exist and what is true, of what has been handed down to us that is worth our keeping. "A whole train of contemplation that takes root and inhabits the mind forever"—of such is the Elephant of the Périgueux Cathedral.

Chapter 3

AT THE LAKE OF TIBERIAS

The second from the last chapter of Belloc's *Places* was written about a trip to the mid-east.[1] In *Places* are essays on Patmos, Syria, Antioch, Damascus, Nazareth, Capharnaum, as well as this essay, "The Lake," which is the Lake of Tiberias or the Sea of Galilee. Clearly, Belloc's visit to this famous place gave him occasion to talk of Christ's presence there.

Belloc tells us that Christ left Nazareth to go to the Sea of Galilee, not too far away, to begin his public life. Here He chose His apostles. Because of Christ's presence there, Belloc notes that this lake is "the most famous sheet of water in the world."

We always find much geography in Belloc. "Nazareth itself stands in the folds of rolling highlands which reach the height of from two to three thousand feet above the sea. . . ." Belloc explains, obviously having walked it himself, that this descent passes by the "broad sward of Hattin."

We might wonder what this "Hattin" is, such is our ignorance of history. Here was "fought one of the most important battles in history, the battle in which the Christians lost the Holy Land, seven hundred and fifty years ago." This battle took place on July 4, 1187. If this is not an approximation, that would make Belloc's visit there to be in 1937, just before World War II.

Belloc graphically tells of this battle in his book, *The Crusades*, which currently may be the most important book we can read to keep up with current events, next perhaps to his chapter on Islam in *The Great Heresies*. Our failure to know and remember the record and theology of Islam may yet prove fatal to us. Few understood this background better than Belloc.

On reading this essay, we can almost see Belloc walking this path from Nazareth. "So at last, at the end of half a day, downwards you come to the shore of the place which gave the Sea of Galilee its Greek and Roman name: the town of Tiberias." Other contemporary travelers had praised this scene as quite beautiful, which it probably is. Belloc, however, knowing its past, tells us that it did not affect him that way.

Everything there carries with it "the air of tragedy," he thought. "Mighty things were done, the greatest of spiritual victories and the triumph of the Resurrection at the end—but I can only believe that the Passion has chiefly imprinted itself upon all that land wherein Our Lord taught, gave the signs from heaven, and suffered, at last, the Agony." A place of tragedy retains the sense of tragedy, somehow.

Belloc never lets us veer too far from reality. We might think that everyone senses the same things that he does. Not at all. "All this (life of Christ) was to fail very quickly in the eyes of the world. It was to last three years; it was to end in a local climax at Jerusalem; it was not to be of very great immediate fame." Few thought at the time of Christ's public life and death that they had made any difference in the world. Sometimes we never know what goes on before our eyes. But "the land has not escaped the stamp of that Deicide."

How did it happen that this land came to be seen as charming? Belloc is sober and philosophic:

> I note also that as the world progressed in its gradual apostasy, as doctrine faded from its intelligence, and as the meaning of all that was here done was lost to it, so did what is called "the modern mind" begin to sentimentalize over the landscape of Judea, and particularly over these waters of the Lake; insisting upon, exaggerating, beauty; when it should rather have had before it the awful business which transformed the world (274–75).

This is a rarely heard insight into the meaning of "modernity" or "the modern mind." Its exaggerated stress on natural beauty is itself a fleeing from what happened in the history of this place.

Belloc looks at the town of Tiberias. He sees much "ruin and desolation" still remaining from its conquest after Hattin. The classic and Christian heritage is gone. "All that loveliness, all that dignity, has gone and the squalor has replaced it which follows everywhere at last the sweep of the Mohammedan conquest." We seldom see these things. When we see them, we dare not speak them. "And that feeling which oppresses every man who goes eastward of the Adriatic comes upon one almost fiercely here on these desolating shores. Ruins . . . ruins . . . ruins" (275). What Belloc saw with his eyes, he comprehended in terms of his mind, in terms of the civilizational effects of different theologies.

But Belloc understands that the Church was, in a way, founded in this very place, where Peter was a fisherman on this Lake. "If you look eastward over the water you see within you the stilling of the storm, and also the Figure passing swiftly over the water to the astonished fishermen upon the boat. That boat, which was the poor possession of Cephas, called also Peter, is a vessel which can never founder; which shall not be cast upon a beach in age and broken up, as other vessels are" (275). On the Lake of Tiberias, what we see is a condition of what we remember, of how we see the world, of what happened in a particular place, at a particular time.

Chapter 4

ON FAME

"People do not really believe that it is important to state the truth upon beauty, that is, upon taste, or even upon any of the works of man," Belloc wrote in a *London Illustrated News* column on St. Valentine's Day, 1920. Belloc at the time was substituting for Chesterton who was traveling in the Near East. Belloc's column is entitled, "The Truth about Modern Art."[1] It is not that no truth can be found in art, nor that people do not have a fairly good idea about what is beautiful and what is not. They just hesitate to speak the truth about it. Referring to the, at the time, newly popular Cubism and Futurism, Belloc thought that the "natural instinct of every man and woman" is, on seeing it, to "protest."

If you are asked what you think of this art, and you state the truth, Belloc thought, you reply, "It is beastly." "That is the highest praise you can give it, while the worst blame you can give it is to say it is childish. If you are not asked for an honest answer but asked to say something courteous, because the perpetrator of the rubbish is related to the person asking you, then, of course, you have to lie" (538). Notice how amusingly Belloc tells us when to "lie"!—No honest answer expected, something courteous, relationship. Thus, we say to the relative, "I like the way the paint sticks to the canvas," or some such vapid response.

The point is not that no truth exists in art but that we hesitate to speak it. Belloc tells us of actually seeing old people carefully examining these new pieces of art. They act the "critic in front of what was, manifestly, to all Gods and men and jackasses, rubbish: stuff which they knew to be rubbish." We need some "light" by which people who see can speak the truth.

A couple of weeks later (March 20, 1920), Belloc returned to a question intimately connected with art, namely, fame, particularly "posthumous fame." We think of great writers, artists, and philosophers who remain famous, even though long dead. The problem that Belloc wonders about is not so much this lasting fame but rather why someone still living would worry about it? Surely Plato and Aristotle are not presently concerned with how many folks read them. This concern for fame is a particular problem, perhaps even a vice, of "noble minds."

Assuming we are indeed dead, and even assuming we are immortal, it does seem odd to think that our main concern in immortality is with whether we are still talked of on earth among those who come long after our time. Belloc recalls that the most celebrated writer who implied that immortal souls might just have some concern for their fame after death was St. Augustine. But the farthest he went "(and he went as far as anybody) was to say that the soul, however blessed, retained the great human affections." Belloc adds that we "hope" this is true, but it is not a "doctrine." Much of what we did at twenty-five, Belloc thinks, we try subsequently, even in this life, at fifty or seventy, to forget. We look back on many of our deeds with a certain gingerness, a certain embarrassment, so why would we want them known down the ages?

Belloc thinks, however, that fame, like hunger and thirst, is a useful thing for the works of man, for without it we would produce little. "The artist, as we all know, does not work for the sake of art, still less for some secret pleasure of his own. He has that pleasure in working. He admires the chance which guides his hand. But his driving motive is fame. It is the driving motive, also of all the failures—that is, of the great mass of men" (560). Fame, the desire for glory about our works and words, motivates us, yet we cannot ourselves know it even if it happens. Even if we praise ourselves, it surely would not, unless we are distinctly odd, be important to us.

Men know, moreover, that fame too early in life is ephemeral and probably won't last long. "It is the longer praise afterwards that they seek." This is the problem. If it is the long-range fame or praise that men seek, fame down the ages, still they will not ever be in a position to know of it or care much about it. In everlastingness, they will, hopefully, be busy with other things. They will not care what earthlings think of them because they will know what earthlings are.

Belloc recounts a delightful story he saw in Max Beerbohm about a poet who sold his soul to the devil for the chance to see what was said of him a hundred years after his death. So, making the deal, he goes to the British Museum. After much search, "he finds one only reference, and that in the shape of a casual allusion made, not in connection with his own work at all, but with another man's work—and in phonetic spelling to boot!" (561).

If we find out what men think of us a century or two after we are dead, it will no doubt be a sobering moment for most of us—some because we are forgotten, some others because we are considered not important, the rest because this fame does not mean much where we now are. The worst would be that we are remembered by posterity mostly for our vices, which we tried carefully to hide in this world.

The French poet, Ronsard, thought that "people who are devout and religious will always write good verse." Belloc was quite astonished at this peculiar doctrine. He adds, "I can hardly remember one thoroughly good man who did write good verse, unless it be the author of the *Pange Lingua*" (i.e., St. Thomas Aquinas). Belloc did not want good men to stop writing inferior verse, nor to prevent bad men from writing good poems.

But because of the pull of this enigmatic fame, we are not to worry. "However bad their verse, you may lay to it that they will go on writing it, in the vain pursuit of posthumous fame" (562). Fame is the judgment of worth that men give to the works and sayings and deeds of those of their kind. It is the human side of praise and worship, of celebration, of indeed what is done in immortality, wherein we praise *what is*. We praise what is, in truth, beautiful.

Belloc recalls in the first essay cited above that a "great sentence comes back into my mind." He gives the sentence in Latin: "*O, Oriens splendor, lucis aeternae, veni et illumina sedentes in tenebris et umbra mortis.*" The paradox of "posthumous fame" is that the greatest effort that we might do, in art, in politics, in philosophy, the record of which we might find in the British Museum long after our death, pales before the "splendor" of the "eternal light." We sit in darkness and in the shadow of death, we with immortal souls with much greater things ahead of us besides our own "posthumous fame." We long, in the end, to affirm, not the fame of what we have done, but openly, honestly, fully, the "truth of beauty."

Chapter 5

"A PLACE WHICH I HAVE NEVER YET SEEN"

Belloc I have long considered simply the best essayist in the English language. I am quite capable of saying the same of Chesterton. In any case, Chesterton is today clearly much better known than Belloc. These two men were great friends; they talked together over much of their respective lifetimes about the highest things and about everything, even about "nothing" as Belloc wrote in a famous essay. In having both their writings we are simply blessed. The opportunity to write something rather regularly on Belloc, as I have for many years on Chesterton in the *Midwest Chesterton News*, is something which I distinctly appreciate.

I have grown skeptical of any idea that a thing is necessarily good because it is well-known. Many well-known things are quite bad. Some of the best things, like, say, the Nicene Creed, are not very well-known even when they are well-known and to be recited every Sunday. We cannot think of Chesterton without in some sense thinking of Belloc. I had always found each in his own way to be a source of delight, wisdom, insight, truth, and, especially in the case of Belloc, of a certain poignancy or nostalgia, that has constantly touched my soul whenever I came across it.

The reader of this book will find me talking about this poignant side of Belloc rather a lot. Belloc was a man who walked and sailed and remembered. This book is not, in form, a scholarly enterprise, nor a matter of historical insight into Belloc's time and writings. I gladly leave that task to others. The good reader will find here the Belloc that moved my soul, the Belloc that brought me to places and to things and to persons I would never have otherwise met or known about. Belloc was a man of this earth in the only way a man can be a man of this earth, by being unsettled in it and by it, especially by its beauty, by the memory of things past, even by the memory of things that might have been otherwise.

My book *Idylls and Rambles: Lighter Christian Essays* contains fifty-four chapters. Why? Because this is the number of essays in J. B. Morton's collection *Selected Essays of Hilaire Belloc*. This wonderful book was actually being discarded from the library of a religious house in San Francisco in which I was living at the time. I retrieved it. The house's loss is definitely my gain.

The fifty-fourth and last essay in the Morton collection is entitled "On Dropping Anchor." The essay begins: "The best noise in all the world is the rattle of the anchor chain when one comes into harbour at last and lets it go over the bows." Now, I am not sailor enough to know this rattling sound, nor why it might be the "best noise in all the world," even though my last name, in German, means "noise" or sound, especially, as I like to think, the sound of a bell.

In sailing one does not always drop anchor, but rather picks up stationary moorings. This means that there is no anchor dropping. But this mooring situation is always precarious, as Belloc recounts in his trying to tie up his boat, the *Silver Star,* at an empty mooring by the Royal Yacht Squadron grounds up the Medina. He had, however, tied up at a rich man's moorings.

According to the custom of courtesy, Belloc recounts, one can "pick up any spare mooring one could find." The rich man, who appeared with his big yacht on the scene, did not think so. Belloc's moral reflection on this incident of the rich man denying his little boat common courtesy was memorable: "Riches, I thought then and I think still, corrupt the heart."

The next tangle with moorings happened to Belloc when he was sailing to Orford town over the bar of the Orford River. Belloc and his companion spotted a buoy and tied up to it, much to the objections of the people on shore. To his surprise, the mooring did not hold his boat. He could not figure out why until he realized that he had tied up to a temporary mooring set up for a rowing regatta, which was why the folks on shore were trying to shout at him not to tie up there. The incident so struck Belloc that he wrote an eighteen line poem about it. "The men that lived in Orford stood / Upon the shore to meet me . . . ."

From this experience, Belloc concludes that it is better to have moorings of one's own, or else to use one's own anchor and hear the chains rattle. This situation of anchors and moorings sets Belloc to further reflection: "I love to consider a place which I have never yet seen, but which I shall reach at last, full of repose and marking the end of those voyages, and security from the tumble of the sea." No wonder Morton chose this essay for the last essay in the Collection!

Belloc then proceeds to imagine such a place that he shall "reach at last." It shall be a cove surrounded by high hills with no houses or signs of men. There should be a little beach and a "breakwater made by God." The tide shall smoothly come in and out of the cove, like a "cup of refreshment and of quiet, a cup of ending." He shall guide his boat up the fairway into the channel and on into the cove that will be cut off from an opening to the sea.

The sea he shall see no more, though he can still hear its noise. All around will be silence. "All alone in such a place, I shall let go the anchor chain, and let it rattle for the last time." He will let the anchor into the clear and salty water, maybe four lengths or more, so that the boat may swing at its anchor. Once secure, he will "tie up (his) canvas and fasten all for the night and get ready for sleep."

This will be the end of Belloc's sailings, in this lovely, imaginary cove, with the steep hills surrounding, the anchor chains finally rattling into the blue, salty water. "And that will be the end of my sailing." The Belloc who sails no more, of course, is the Belloc who has finally come home into his cove, who has finished with what delights and dreams this world has given to him in his *Silver Star*.

Let me repeat again these nostalgic, memorable words: "I love to consider a place which I have never yet seen, but which I shall reach at last, full of repose and marking the end of those voyages, and security from the tumble of the sea." This is the human condition. We live in a world that makes us love to consider a place we have not yet seen, a place that we shall reach at last. The "end" of Belloc's sailing is, after all, our end, isn't it?

Part 2

"Of Courtesy, it is much less
Than Courage of Heart or Holiness,
Yet in my Walks it seems to me
That the Grace of God is in Courtesy."

—Hilaire Belloc, "Courtesy," *Sonnets and Verse*, 1923.

Chapter 6

THE PATH TO ROME:
BELLOC'S WALK A CENTURY LATER

"To every honest reader that may purchase, hire, or receive this book, and to the reviewers also (to whom it is of triple profit), greeting—and whatever else can be had for nothing."

—Hilaire Belloc, *The Path to Rome*[1]

"And now all you people reading, may have read, or shall in the future read this my many-sided but now ending book; and all of you also that in the mysterious designs of Providence may not be fated to read it for some very long time to come . . . the time is come when I must bid you farewell."

—Hilaire Belloc, *The Path to Rome*[2]

I.

In the Year 1901, the English essayist, historian, poet, sailor, and traveler, Hilaire Belloc (1870–1953), decided to make a pilgrimage from Toul in France, scene of his military training in the French army, to the Eternal City. He chose a direct path to Rome, or at least as direct as the mountains and rivers of Europe would allow him to walk that distance in a straight line. He vowed—for a pilgrimage was a sacred event in the tradition of Christian men—that he would walk every step of the way in the same boots with which he began, that he would hear Mass every morning, that he would not take a wheeled vehicle, and that he would

29

arrive in Rome on the Feast of Sts. Peter and Paul (29 June) in time for Mass in the great Basilica of St. Peter's.

Needless to say, Belloc broke all the elements of his vow except its final one. He did make it to Rome, though when he arrived, he told us practically nothing of what he saw there.

> "Well, as a pilgrimage cannot be said to be over till the first Mass is heard in Rome, I have twenty minutes to add to my book." So, passing an Egyptian obelisk which the great Augustus had nobly dedicated to the Sun, I entered. . . . LECTOR: "But do you intend to tell us nothing of Rome?" AUCTOR: "Nothing, dear Lector." LECTOR: "Tell me at least one thing; did you see the Coliseum?" AUCTOR: ". . . I entered a café at the right hand of a very narrow, long, straight street, called for bread, coffee, and brandy. . . ."[3]

Belloc then writes as his concluding words in the book, presumably from the same café, a "Dithyrambic Epithalamium on Threnody," the concluding lines of which read: "Across the valleys and the high-land / With all the world on either hand / Drinking when I had a mind to, / Singing when I felt inclined to; / Nor ever turned my face to home / Till I had slaked my heart at Rome." The Lector calls this "doggerel," but Belloc does not mind. His walk is ended, his vow completed.

The Path to Rome is thus not about Rome but about getting there through a Europe that reflects Rome, Empire and Church, at every step. Belloc passed along the Rhone, over the Alps, through Switzerland, the Apennines, and into the Italian plains and cities on his path. As he went along, he told us much. He told us especially much of himself. Belloc, I think, could see more about something than most of us even when we are looking at the same thing. It is not merely that our memory is a function of what we see, so likewise is our hope, so likewise is our present being.

Not unlike Plato in *The Apology of Socrates*, Belloc was conscious of the fact that this account of his walk would be read down the ages. In this sense, his "path" is a walk we can all take. Because he recounted his trek in a book, we can still take the same walk. We could not do this even if we set off tomorrow morning from Toul to Rome by ourselves, with our staff and our boots and our vows. Our walk would not be his. I am sure that there are a number of people in the twentieth and twenty-first centuries who have or who will actually take Belloc's walk. They will have in their pocket his book as a guide-book. They will begin from Toul and end in Rome, even on the Feast of Sts. Peter and Paul. I envy them. They will try to eat and drink what he ate and drank where he ate and drank it. But "in divine Providence,"" as he calls it, this newer walk, for all its attention to place, weather, local characteristics, drawings, and scenery, will not see what Belloc saw. Belloc's book is an account of spirit, yes, of a spirit very much embodied in matter.

Belloc has no Manichean tendencies, of course, nor even any Platonic tendencies that would see the whole man in his spirit or in his soul, though he does have a soul that connects him with *what is*.

> In early youth the soul can still remember its immortal habitation, and clouds and edges of hills are of another kind from ours, and every scent and colour has a savour of Paradise. . . . Youth came up that valley of evening, borne upon a settled state, and their now sudden influence upon the soul in short ecstasies is the proof that they stand outside time, and are not subject to decay. This, then, was the blessing of Sillano (a small Italian town he had reached), and here was perhaps the highest moment of those seven hundred miles—or more.[4]

The things that "stand outside of time," the things that can be "had for nothing," the ability to recognize our "highest moment" —such are the important things that make us what we are, things that we might miss on our own walks from Toul to Rome or wherever we might wander if we do not first spend time with Belloc on his walk.

We know more about *The Path to Rome*, as a book, if we realize that, in the following year, 1902, Belloc took another walk in his native Sussex in England, where he intimates that the original Garden of Eden was located. "The north is the place for men. Eden was there, and the four rivers of Paradise are the Seine, the Ouse, the Thames, and the Arun, there are grasses there, and the trees are generous, and the air is an unnoticed pleasure."[5] What a remarkable phrase—"an unnoticed pleasure!" We are such earthlings that we think that we notice all our pleasures. Belloc confesses that "I was not made for Tuscany."

31

This second 1902 walk, equally as charming as the 1901 *Path to Rome*, was called *The Four Men*. Needless to say, each of the men on this latter excursion was Belloc himself. I have followed this English walk in an earlier chapter (Chapter 1). Suffice it to say here that both walks were lonely affairs and therefore ironically both profound lessons in companionship. To know one another, indeed to love one another, we also need silence, to be alone, the gift of the contemplative tradition. Those who have no silence, who do not sometimes walk alone, have no friends. Yet, *The Path to Rome* is full of Belloc's affirmations that, after long stretches by himself, he suddenly "has need of companionship."

II.

Belloc is often reviled for his famous sentence that "Europe is the faith and the faith is Europe." I cannot number the times that I have seen this sentence cited with horror and derision—and with much superficiality of understanding about what he meant by it. Yet, there is a truth to it that can be seen in this walk from Toul to Rome in the late Spring and early Summer of 1901, a walk that took Belloc over the Jura and the Alps in the snow, while traversing the plains of France and Italy in such heat that he mostly walked at night and slept by day wherever he could, sometimes in inexpensive inns, sometimes in a barn, often in the open under a tree or in the shade of bushes. He finds crosses and small chapels on the mountains. He sees the gentle hospitality of men in pubs and peasant women in serving him breakfast. He buys a good wine that sometimes tastes sour to him in the morning. We can feel his hunger and the delight of the fresh loaves that he finds in the little house that is the baker's, the one pointed out to him that has smoke coming out of the chimney early in the morning. Bakers, he thinks, are the finest of men because they have to arise so early and thus see the day come to be.

Belloc is adamantly "incarnational," that is, he does not separate the soul and the body. There is much in *The Path to Rome* about food and wine and sleep, as I have already intimated, almost as if it is all right to be the kind of beings we are. "It is quite clear that the body must be recognized and the soul kept in its place, since a little refreshing food and drink can do so much to make a man."[6] Belloc is always aware of the truth that Augustine knew that the great temptations, the great crimes, do not arise from the flesh but, as in the case of Lucifer himself, from the spirit. And even when they appear in the flesh, they usually, in some way obscure but reflectively traceable in us, are controlled by the spirit.

Yet, we are beings with a certain sadness about us. Poignancy is found in every work of Belloc, even in his laughter and amusement, of which there is much. "Then let us love one another and laugh. Time passes, and we shall laugh no longer—and meanwhile common living is a burden, and earnest men are at siege upon us all around. Let us suffer absurdities, for that is only to suffer one another."[7] We are under siege. What we believe in the faith of Europe is rejected openly more than a hundred years after Belloc's walk. But we laugh. We are indeed absurdities. Suffering one another is not merely a suffering; it is also patience, a world full of laughter.

Early in his walk to Rome, to give a further example of his thinking on food, Belloc asks about breakfast. His very way of asking the question is delightful. "I would very much like to know what those who have an answer to everything can say about the food requisite to breakfast?"[8] "Those who have an answer for everything," we suspect, have, in Belloc's mind, few answers to anything. He recalls that Marlowe, Jonson, Shakespeare, and Spenser drank beer for breakfast plus a little bread. In his French regiment, he remembers, for breakfast they drank black coffee "without sugar," with a cut of a stale piece of bread to go with it.

The great (French) Republicans fought first and ate later. Belloc was also a sailor and ate "nothing for several hours." He continues:

> Dogs eat the first thing they come across, cats take a little milk, and gentlemen are accustomed to get up at nine and eat eggs, bacon, kidneys, ham, cold pheasant, toast, coffee, tea, scones, and honey, after which they will boast that their race is the hardiest in the world and ready to bear every fatigue in the pursuit of Empire. But what rule governs all of this? Why is breakfast different from all other things, so that the Greeks called it the best thing in the world . . .?[9]

How amusing is this description of the breakfast of the hearty and hardy English gentleman, with its four meats plus eggs, in pursuit of Empire and oblivious of fatigue! And what was Greece if not a constant search for precisely "the best thing in the world"?

In re-reading *The Path to Rome*, what struck me was Belloc's sense that the authority of God was put into the world to unsettle us, that we could be here much too occupied with ourselves, that we really did not want to bother with revelation, especially if it meant any kind of revolution in our manners or in our morals.

> For when boys or soldiers or poets, or any other blossoms and prides of nature, are for lying steady in the shade and letting the Mind commune with its Immortal Comrades, up comes Authority busking about and eager as though it were a duty to force the said Mind to burrow and sweat in the matter of this very perishable world, its temporary habitation. "Up," says Authority, "and let me see that Mind of yours doing something practical. Let me see Him mixing painfully with circumstance, and botching up some Imperfection or other that shall at least be a Reality and not a silly Fantasy."[10]

These are profound, if diverting words.

The temporary habitation of the mind can be quite pleasant to it. Why worry about anything else? It is best to lay "steady in the shade," to dream of worlds that perhaps might be, fantasies, to be sure. Authority is something of a pest. Yet, there are things that Mind prefers not to pay attention to, the first of which is Reality itself. How well does Belloc describe the men of our kind who are wont to favor their own musings over a more glorious reality that they could only receive, but not invent by themselves!

Chapter 7

PERMANENCE

After I had read Belloc's essay on "Permanence" in *The Silence of the Sea*, a copy of which my friend Gregory Doolan let me borrow from his Belloc collection, I came across this passage in Belloc's essay "On Diarists":

> Why are there so few diaries? Because mankind, and even womankind, lacks the industry required. Most people have enough routine in their lives and certainly enough leisure to keep up the daily entries; but they have not the tenacity sufficient to keep abreast of the work. For one thing, there is no money in it. And yet I suppose that every man who has lived a long life, especially if it is a half-public sort, regrets his lack of a diary. However wrong-headed his judgments may have been, however superficial his appreciations, he would have preserved out of ten thousand chance happenings a hundred or two which would have been of permanent value to him.

How does Belloc understand what is "permanent"?

One of the permanent things seems to be how little we remember about ourselves, itself perhaps an argument for the existence of a heaven, of a God who delights even in our wrong-headed judgments and our superficial appreciations, not because they are wrong-headed or superficial but because they were ours, the immortal creature in his path through this world. Our sins and wrong-headed judgments are not only to be forgiven, but learned from, even in retrospect laughed at. They are not valueless.

Obviously, Belloc allows that not everything that happens to us is necessarily of permanent importance. I wonder if we understand the implication of this freedom we have to allow many insignificant things to happen to us in our everyday lives. We brush our teeth every day, but we need not be so vain as to think that this needs recording for posterity, even though one or other brushing may well turn out to be of permanent amusement, the day that we used shaving cream instead of toothpaste, for example.

Moreover, our mothers once asked us every day during our early youth whether we brushed our teeth before we went to bed or after we got up. Someone revealed an interest in us, in the most boring things about us, not because it was so exciting watching us brush our teeth—though watching children brush their teeth can be most entertaining, but because our mother knew what was important was the ten thousand daily brushings, the regularity, the routine, the permanent recurrence of ordinary things.

In his essay on "Permanence," Belloc, reflecting on the many changes after the Great War, noted the "Permanency of Impermanence." This experience gives us a certain strength. "Though you may not affirm of any one thing in the mortal world that it is permanent, yet you may affirm of Permanence itself that it is permanent. You may repeat to yourself with confidence that the principle of permanence underlies all vicissitude." Spring and Fall return each year. These natural cycles, with the heavens, are not technically eternal, yet they are "in tune" with it and they are "a promise thereof."

Belloc finds the "principal value of history" in this experience of permanence in change. Not only do we have our immediate contact with the ten thousand things of daily life, we add a "third dimension" with this historical experience. History shows us "the limits to which the most generous enthusiasms must be confined, the term beyond which the most just of reforms may not venture, and the minimum at least of evil which human society must learn to endure." Notice what is said here, that generous enthusiasms can be excessive, that just reform can turn unjust, that we cannot get rid of all evil without increasing it. In other words, we are to pay attention to the limits of our condition.

History is the record of the importance of "accident" in our lives. And yet it also teaches the permanence of things that recur. Belloc recalls once in "Barbary," in Algeria perhaps under the Atlas Mountains, where he saw a farmer plow his fields in the evening.

Belloc knew that this "landscape" before him and the farmer had seen "every sort of revolution." The pagan gods and the signs of Christian presence, "all these had gone their way." Yet, the sun went down and would return. "With the morning there would be a new prayer in gratitude for the sun's rising and life advancing from the east, and the ploughing of the field would begin anew." Belloc, aware of the history of the place, was reminded of things that are permanent.

However, even this recurrent ritual "of man and earth will go its way at last, after we know not what aeons of time." To a man who is overcome with the woes of his era, Belloc advises him to look again at these rhythms of ploughing and planting. "High verse" has this same effect, he thought. "Any civilisation must be near its end when its cities outweigh its country-sides." And yet, we notice that as the cities grow, in a sense so does the countryside. The two are not necessarily opposed to one another but require one another; indeed, cause one another.

And of the most recurrent of temporal things, Belloc writes: "The Heavens, which are so much more ancient and will outlast that which they roof, are not themselves for ever, but they have 'for ever' written large upon them, for all men to read, and having read, to make seizing (ownership) of their own dignity and of their immortal destinies. We, part of their household, may on that account repeat without fear that the immemorial hills, the deep woods, and the quiet rivers shall return." That is a remarkable and remarkably beautiful sentence by any standards. The heavens, that "roof" us, will outlast us, but they too are not "forever."

Yet, their recurring permanence has "forever" written on them for us "to read." And after we read what is there, we can take possession of our own dignity and of our "immortal destiny." Our unwritten diaries would be filled with our recollections of the hills and woods and rivers we have seen and visited, wherein the ten thousand unimportant and one or two hundred important things of our lives took place. We are part of the household of the heavens in which we are to read and take possession of our dignity and our destiny.

Chapter 8

ON THE VANITY OF THE LEARNED MAN

Belloc's *The Cruise of the Nona*, his account of skippering his sturdy little boat around England, is a book that I have not read in ages. However, one day a month or so ago, I was coming back to the Rosslyn Metro Station across the Potomac in Virginia. I happened to have with me the collection, *Hilaire Belloc's Stories, Essays and Poems,* which Gregory Doolan had let me borrow from his fine Belloc collection. This book extracted some twenty-two pages from *The Cruise of the Nona.*

Belloc did everything with great zest and great style. His cruises, his walks, his journeys, his accounts of wars and places were, however, ever filled with philosophic reflection, with wonderment about why and how things happen to our kind. The *Nona*, sailing north in late May out of Holyhead harbor, ran into a swift and unexpected gale at the point of Caernarvonshire going into Bardsey Sound. Belloc was not sure if he was afraid or not, so busy did the storm occupy him. Finally, he and his companion got the battered *Nona* past the Black Rock, the Carrick Dhu, into smoother water away from the surging tide.

Looking about, Belloc saw that he was in a rather famous historical spot. This caused him to wonder about theories of learned men trying to expound the history of where he was. "One of the saddest things I know about the beach near Bideford River is the deadly hatred with which the Dons have devastated poor, dear Kenwith."

What, we wonder, have the Dons done that was so unjust to "dear Kenwith"? Why did they hate it so? Evidently, Kenwith is the place of early Danish landings—"a few boatloads"—in England. The oral tradition and local history all attest to the place where this landing took place. The learned scholars, it seems, refuse this tradition. They call it a "popular error," and locate the landing some miles away. At this point,

Belloc decides that he wants to analyze this tendency of the academics not to believe local tradition or witness.

"What are their motives?" he wonders of the academics. The thing happens in all countries and in all universities, "but one is puzzled why it should come into being at all." These are the same folks, Belloc recalls, who say that the Gospel of John was not written by John, or that Homer did not write Homer, or that "the Battle of Hastings was not called the Battle of Hastings—although the people who fought it there called it the Battle of Hastings." These same Dons also think that Caesar's *Gallic Wars* was written by his tutor—"and all the rest of the nonsense." No doubt, Belloc's own unpleasant experience with the university is reflected here.

This force that causes academic Dons to "make fools of themselves," Belloc thinks, can be reduced to three basic elements: 1) "First of all there is the vanity of the learned man." Since so few other scholars know about the situation, the learned man can get by with false conclusions without too much notice. The vain Don likes to think himself right and all the normal clods wrong. Today there is such a mass of technical evidence that people will swallow almost anything.

2) The second reason for their making fools of themselves is the "love of the marvelous, though it is a love of the marvelous appearing in a very degraded form." Belloc gives this example of how the love of the marvelous works to distort the facts:

> Your pedant says: "All the apparent evidence, all tradition, all that you would call common sense, would make out Little Muddipool to be that same Little Muddipool where the treaty of Little Muddipool was signed. It is called in plain words. 'The Treaty of Little Muddipool,' and its last words are 'Made by us at Little Muddipool.' But *I* tell you that it was not Little Muddipool at all, but a place a hundred miles away with a different name.

The love of the marvelous, the desire of uniqueness, causes the scholar to ignore common sense and his own experience. No one will think it marvelous to learn that the Treaty of Little Muddipool was signed in a place called Little Muddipool. But it you tell everyone that it was signed actually in Liverpool, against all the common sense evidence, they will take notice.

3) The third reason is negative. It is the "perpetual substitution of hypothesis for fact." This tendency Belloc finds to be "the greatest mark of Dons today." With this attitude of mind, the Dons find that they cannot "weigh the proportion of evidence." Hypotheses make all sorts of results possible, in spite of the evidence. The "certain, the probable, and the absurd" can thus be no longer distinguished.

And to show how modern Belloc is, he recalls a case in his time at Oxford of a Don who claimed that he had "discovered any number of classical passages containing concealed anagrams, furnishing the most astonishing information; for instance, that Euripides, when he was a little boy, wrote the plays of Aeschylus." Were this so, of course, the Oxford Don, as Belloc put it, would be responsible for a "miracle."

Fortunately, Belloc recalls, this sort of nonsense was put a stop to by another gentleman writing to *The Spectator* who pointed out that he had used the anagram method on the said Don's name, only to discover that it was but "a thinly concealed anagram in the opening lines of the *Iliad*." This proved, on his own theory, that the Oxford Don must have written the *Iliad* not merely when he was a little boy, "but long before he was born."

Belloc's amusing conclusion of these reflections on learned men, while he is tied up in little shallows in Bardsey Sound, is "and so much for that."

What perhaps makes this witty account of the foibles of the academic Dons rather pertinent is Belloc's perception that "the certain, the probable, and the absurd" are today difficult to distinguish because we no longer easily know how to distinguish hypotheses from facts. Belloc thought that the common man living near Kenwith, insisting that the Danes landed near Kenwith, as their ancestors had handed it down, or that the Treaty of Little Muddipool took place at Little Muddipool, is generally close to the truth.

The hypotheses of the Dons prove something approaching the absurd because they marveled at their own theories more than the facts. The greatest mark of the Dons today does indeed seem to be the "substitution of hypothesis for fact," the systematic reduction of *what is* into what might be and the subsequent difficulty in discovering any difference between the two.

Chapter 9
ARS TAEDICA

My friend Gregory Doolan, as I have mentioned, has an excellent collection of Belloc books. He did not have, however, the last time I checked, many of Belloc's books of essays, none of the "On" books, for example, though he does have a couple of different collections of Belloc's shorter pieces. Normally, I hesitate to borrow a book I genuinely covet. But finally, without necessarily revealing this darker side of my own otherwise happy nature—I figure ex-students should be smart enough to have already figured it out—I borrowed, as I mentioned in the previous chapter, Hilaire Belloc, *Stories, Essays, and Poems*.[1]

The book that Doolan had was a 1957 hardback, an enlarged reprint copy, the Everyman's Library Edition, with an Introduction by J. B. Morton. On the title page, the book bears the name of "Francis Sample, Cathedral College." I have no idea where Cathedral College might be. Doolan must have found this collection in a used book store someplace. If there is anything I like to see in ex-students of mine, besides their being aware of the darker sides of human nature, including my own, it is a diligence in haunting used book stores.

Two days after I borrowed this book, I took it with me to read on the Washington Metro returning to the Rosslyn Station across the Potomac from Georgetown. The first short piece I read was called "Mrs. Markham on the Police." It was really a funny account of a certain Mrs. Markham talking to her children. One of my Denver cousins in fact is a "Mrs. Markham," but bears no other similarity to this English lady explaining to her children why we have police, even though, in England, they only can use truncheons.

"No, my dear, we (English) do not give them (police) arms because we think it would be cruel and unjust. But we let them have a thick stick called a truncheon, with which they can hit people upon the head as hard as ever they like, to make them obey." You will understand the high metaphysical quality of Belloc's work by the next question Mrs. Markham's son Tommy asks her, "What do they do, Mamma, when, after the policemen have hit and hit and hit with their truncheons, and yet people will not obey?" This is a query worthy of an Augustine.

The second item I read was an essay entitled "The Art of Boring." I must confess almost breaking into tears on the Metro as I read it, so funny it was. I am conscious of the outlandish effect on other absorbed Metro riders when an elderly gentleman bursts sporadically into laughter while reading an otherwise innocuous-looking book. I still get what are called "giggles" when I think about it.

What made the essay doubly funny to me, as I read it, was its similarity of thesis to what is known as the Reverse Peter Principle. The Peter Principle, to recall, states, more or less, that we rise to the level of our incompetence so that, in effect, every job is filled by an incompetent. This is a principle that, more than others I have seen, helps to explain our current political scene.

However, let us suppose that, by manipulating this principle, you are shrewd enough to prevent yourself from rising to the level of your own incompetence. You simply want to stay at a level you are comfortable with. The way you do it is, on the occasion of your being considered to be Department Head or Associate Vice President or District Manager, you manage to do something so outlandish, like, say, suddenly cut off all your hair, or you begin to light your pipe with a sunglass. On observing your behavior, the already incompetents in charge quietly pass you over.

Belloc's "Art of Boring" is not unmindful of and probably was inspired by the famous essay of the Roman poet Horace's satire on "The Bore" and on how difficult it is to get rid of him. This is where Belloc suggests that what he is talking about, in Latin, is "*Ars Taedica*"—*taedium* means weariness or loathing, hence boring. What is at issue for Belloc is not whether you yourself are boring to others, but whether you can deliberately be boring to others, either to pay them back or to accomplish some other worthy purpose. This is the similarity to the Reverse Peter Principle.

"The Art of Boring" is a handbook on how to go about boring other people. Belloc tells us that many books and essays are written complaining of bores, but he recalls none to tell us how to acquire this useful art. Many bores, of course, are unconscious of the quality of their ability to bore other people to death. But positively to choose to bore, you must practice and have some skill. There are rules for boring others.

First you have to recognize the signs that the phenomenon is present. "The first sign is an attention in the eye of the bored person to something trivial other than yourself." You will notice the genius of Belloc's writing when you try to ask whether the pronoun "yourself" here was deliberately intended to refer also to "something trivial." To make his point, Belloc remarks that "if while you are talking to him his eye is directed to a person aiming a gun at him that is not a sign of boredom."

On the other hand, if his eye is caught by a "little bird" or "a passing cloud," this is a sign that he is bored with you. Two other signs of boredom are: 1) when the other keeps interspersing interjections that have nothing to do with what you are talking about, and 2) when the bored person suddenly begins to talk to someone else in the midst of your discourse with him.

Just as any topic can be made boring, so can any topic be made interesting. The trick is to know how to make something vitally interesting to be dull. One way is the monotonous tone of your voice. A second way is to bring in a lot of useless detail and to branch off into all directions. Belloc gives the following example of hesitating over a date as a brilliant way for someone who wants to bore another to proceed: "'It was in July 1921—no, now I come to think of it, it must have been 1920, because—' (then tell them why it must have been 1920). 'No, now I think of it, it must have been 1921' (then tell them why it was 1921)—'or was it 1922? Anyway, it was July, and the year doesn't matter; the whole point is the month.'" Belloc calls this simply "a capital beginning, especially the last words, which indicate to the bored one that you have deliberately wasted his time to no purpose."

We make the same boring approach with a name, or by introducing many superfluous words and adjectives. Moral and artistic digressions are also helpful in boring someone to death. Belloc's reasonings here are enormously amusing: "Stop in the middle of the thing and add to the agony by explaining that you don't mind a man's getting drunk, or that you do mind it, or that you have no objections to such building as you are describing, or what not: for your private opinions in art and morals are the most exquisitely boring things in the world and you can't bring them up too much." A particularly fine way to bore someone else, Belloc adds, is to forget the end of a story you are telling. You could also led your listener up to a major question and ask eloquently, "What do you think to be the answer?" Then you forget the answer.

Belloc addresses the case of people who are adept at recognizing our boringness so that they try to defend themselves against it. It takes considerable skill on the part of the borer to defeat this sort of counter-attack by the boree. Suppose the borer is speaking dryly and at length of Rio to the bored listener. The latter fights back by announcing that he too knows Rio. He then starts giving back what he knows to the borer. How does the one intending to bore deflect such a one approach? Two ways are open. One is to complain that you are being interrupted. The other is to wait till the other's knowledge of Rio is exhausted, and then continue right on as before.

A skilled defender against a boring person can also try this: he can wait patiently till the borer (who, remember, is deliberately trying to bore) finishes his point. The bored man can wait a moment and then ask the bore to go on, as if he had not known the boring story was finished. The proper way to defend against this defense, Belloc thinks, is for the one inflicting the boring story simply to repeat it.

If the boree tries to walk away from the borer, it will often work, but this is a sign of defeat. The borer's proper response, and it takes a brave man to do this, is to follow the bored man walking away, corner him, and continue with the boring story as if nothing has happened.

Belloc gives two fine points about how to be boring. The first is to put long pauses into one's conversations and dare the other to break it. Just as the boree is about to interrupt, recommencing the boring story. "The other way is talking half incomprehensibly, mumbling, and the rest of it—then, when the boree impatiently asks you to repeat, do it still less clearly." This method, Belloc adds, "never fails."

In the end, Belloc thinks that this fine art of boring others (*ars taedica*) probably cannot be learned with rules and precepts. Then he adds, with exquisite irony in the light of all that he has said about names and dates, "perhaps I have written in vain." That is to say, in setting out deliberately to bore us with an essay on "the art of boring," he has in fact delighted us by reminding us how utterly boring we can be.

Chapter 10

ON THE USEFULNESS OF THE NEW YEAR

Belloc remarks, in an essay entitled, "On New Years and New Moons" (*The Silence of the Sea*), that many different kinds of New Year's celebrations and datings can be found. Once the New Year began on "Lady's Day," March 25th. The Hebrews and the Chinese have differing dates for the New Year. Then there is the calculations that changed things a bit with establishment of the Julian and Gregorian Calendars.

But mostly, Belloc reflects, "The New Year is over-valued. Properly speaking, it is not there at all. It is a whimsy; it is an imaginary; it is a fiction of the mind; it is a convention; it is a fraud." In fact, Belloc cannot figure out why those who "object to anything that is not tangible and can be tested by experience" have not protested against the arbitrary imagination that says that the New Year begins on January 1, when it could in fact begin at any time we choose.

Belloc compares the New Year to the New Moon which he says at least is "something real." The New Moon, he continues, "hangs in the sky a tender crescent." My dictionary does not give the New Moon as the Crescent, of waxing or waning, but of the complete dark moon when its face is full to the Sun.

In any case, "the New Moon is worthy of our adoration because she is real." Then Belloc adds a bit of metaphysics and epistemology: "The light on that lovely little, exiguous little, gradually brightening little arc is real, if, indeed, anything told us by our sense be real." Thus, we can hold the New Moon is real even if we cannot touch it, though our kind have walked on it since Belloc wrote. Notice that Belloc, knowing about Kant, implicitly recognizes that there are those who deny that our mind through senses can get to the real. Thus, we must postulate the real, lest they walk about in a world that they deny exists.

But Belloc's main point is about the New Year. "I say that the New Year is a whimsy; an imaginary; a nothing." If we do celebrate the New Year, it is because it is "part of the myth-making of man." Seasons, to be sure, do change, days grow longer and shorter "after Goodwood." I wondered what this "Goodwood" was. It was not in my desk dictionary, nor in the *Oxford English Dictionary*. Obviously it means Midsummer's Night in some way, after which the days begin to be shorter. But here we have Belloc pointing out that something is a whimsy, yet, at the same time, that we can have rites and ceremonies about it. And what is the purpose of the rites surrounding New Year?

"A New Year has this useful thing about it, whether it be Mohammedan, Hebrew, Julian, Gregorian, Chinese, or Choctaw. It makes man remember and regret his follies and his sins." I need to point out that it is a different thing to regret our sins and to regret our follies. The rite for dealing with the former is much better established than that dealing with the latter. Sins can be forgiven; our follies are often never forgotten.

Men with few sins can have many follies, while great sinners can be relatively free of follies. Yet, Belloc reminds us, both are to be acknowledged. This passage, indeed, reminds me of a line of Chesterton who said, if I recall it correctly, that "we can be sorry for our sins but not for spilling gravy on our ties in a fine restaurant." The latter is not a sin, but it is a folly. We do regret the bad figure we cut with gravy stains on our ties.

Thus, when a man comes to the end of his days, Belloc thinks, "on the downward slope" where he sees "the marble tomb," he sees on either side of him these two companions, follies and sins. "They talk to him continually." He says to himself, in my words, "Oh no! of this folly" and "God forgive me of that sin."

Our follies and our sins need to be reckoned with. If we do not deal with them, "we should make very poor wayfaring with them at the end." When we do come to the end, we notice that we have lost the "other friends and fellowships." What we have left are our follies and our sins. We even strike up a conversation with ourselves, Belloc thinks: "Good morning, my dear Folly Number 8!" Then he feels his sleeve being pulled for attention, and responds: "Good morning, Sin Number 368. Remember me to all the little sins."

I do not know whether the fact that Belloc mentions 368 sins and only eight follies is significant. I would be loathe to think that such is the proportion between follies and sins in most normal lives, though I would not be surprised. But notice that Belloc does not make New Year's Resolutions on this arbitrary day, enhanced by much ceremonial. "I say that at the New Year we enter into preparatory companionship with our follies and our sins. Wherefore idiots on this occasion make good resolutions."

Belloc thinks we had best not calculate what we might promise ourselves to do, but rather take an account of what we have done. We are better off to "make money (which lasts) or hay while the sun shines," than New Year's resolutions. But, of course, from Scripture, we know, as does Belloc, that money does not last, though it usually lasts longer than our good resolutions. Besides, the sun does not shine "at the New Year, and there is no hay, except what is already stacked under its thatch in the rick outside the yard."

What does this mean? It means that the sun does not shine on New Year and there is no hay, except that already stacked? It means that we best reckon with our follies and our sins, however many be their number. Unlike our resolutions, they are real and impinge on our souls. If we do not deal with them, our good resolutions will make little difference and will only translate into further follies and sins. Thus, if the New Year is a fiction and a fancy and does not exist at all, it does not follow that the same can be said of our sins and follies, whatever their number might be.

Part 3

"The Catholic Church is an institution of necessity autonomous. It cannot admit the right of any other power exterior to its own organization to impose upon it a modification of its discipline or, above all, a new conception of its hieratic organization. The reader must carefully distinguish between the acceptation by the Church of a detail of economic reform, the consent to suppress a corporation at the request of the civil power, or even to forgo certain traditional political rights, and the admission of the general principles of control."

—Hilaire Belloc, *The French Revolution,* 1911, 241–42.

Chapter 11

"ISLAM WILL NOT BE THE LOSER"

"Islam has not suffered this spiritual decline (as in the West); and in the contrast between the religious certitudes still strong throughout the Mohammedan world, as lively in India as in Morocco, active throughout North Africa and Egypt, even inflamed through contrast and the feeling of repression in Syria—more particularly in Palestine—lies our peril . . . .

"These lines are written in the month of January, 1937; perhaps before they appear in print the rapidly developing situation in the Near East will have marked some notable change. Perhaps that change will be deferred, but change there will be, continuous and great. *Nor* does it seem probable that at the end of such a change, especially if the process be prolonged, *Islam will be the loser*."

—Hilaire Belloc, *The Crusades.*[1]

"Of course this (attack on World Trade Center) is 'about Islam.' The question is, what exactly does that mean? For a vast number of 'believing' Muslim men, 'Islam' stands, in a jumbled, half-examined way, not only for the fear of God, but also for a cluster of customs, opinions and prejudices that include . . . a more particularized loathing and fear of the prospect that their own immediate surroundings could be taken over—'Westoxicated'—by the liberal Western-style way of life . . . . The restoration of religion to the sphere of the personal, its depoliticization, is the nettle that all Muslim societies must grasp in order to become modern. If terrorism is to be defeated, the world of Islam must take on board the secularist-humanist principles on which the modern is based, and without which Muslim countries' freedom will remain a distant dream."

—Salman Rushdie, *The New York Times.*

"Islam is the most dynamic force today because, unlike other major religions, it hasn't succumbed to secularism. It doesn't divide human life between the religious and the secular, the spiritual and the totality of human existence. Only Islam is the route to victory."

—Mahmoud Ahmad Ghazi.[2]

I.

Understanding Islam's force and success was, and is, a great intellectual, cultural, and, yes, theological mystery. Today Islam controls about one-fifth of the population of the globe with some twenty-five nations stretching from Morocco to Afghanistan and south to Indonesia and much of northern and central Africa. Some decades after the fall of communism, when we expected to have no further "world-historical" problems, we find a remarkably vigorous and often militant Islam at our very doorsteps.

What are we to make of this surprising confrontation with Islam? One could maintain that no one saw its coming so far in advance better than the English historian and writer Hilaire Belloc, who understood the global interests and ambitions of an Islam never content to be confined within its own historic borders. In today's world, however, we are accustomed to distinguish between a certain minority of Islamic "terrorists" and the vast majority of Muslims who are said to be "peaceful," these latter themselves often, as in Afghanistan, subject to these same terrorists.

Whether this analysis is adequate, however politically correct it is, remains to be seen. Belloc certainly thought the potential problem of Islam is not confined to a small minority of "terrorists" or "militants" who stand wholly outside its own system. It is difficult to see why such terrorists are not arising within the system. This is, at least, what they believe of themselves.

Why Belloc's reflections on Islam are worthwhile recalling today, however, is because he asked a question that is seldom brought up today, namely, "what is Islam?" What is its theology? What is its common core? Of all the world religions, it has proved to be the most closed to outside influence. Converts from Islam to Christianity or to any other religion almost never happen. It appears as a completely closed system enforced by both custom, law, and, not to be underestimated, coercion. It has grown largely through conquest or, in recent times, by relative population growth against a West bent on depopulating itself.

In modern times, Islam has been divided into many differing states, often at odds with each other, though in all there is, in practice, a union of Mosque and state, however defined in each one. We find no single religious authority to define just what Islam holds in the light of its many differing interpretations of itself. Certainly a case can be made that the "terrorist" version is legitimate, as it claims to be. There is, however, no credible large-scale Islamic army with sophisticated technology. What weapons, including nuclear technology, Islamic armies have were purchased from the West or East, usually with oil money. Even this military capacity is generally considered to be second-class, at best.

It was not always so. In much of the middle ages, Islamic forces were the best armed and organized in the world. But since the victory at the Battle of Vienna—a date that Belloc gives as September 11, 1683[3]—Islamic forces have not been united or able to resist better organized military power.

"Since then the armed power of Mohammedanism has declined," Belloc wrote.

> "But neither its numbers nor the convictions of its followers have
> appreciably declined; and as in the territory annexed by it, though
> it has lost places in which it ruled over subject Christian majorities,

it has gained new adherents—to some extent in Asia, and largely in Africa. Indeed, in Africa it is still expanding among the Negroid populations, and that expansion provides an important future problem for the European Governments who have divided Africa between them."[4]

Since these words were written, of course, no European colonial powers are in control in Africa or in Asia, while the Muslim states along the southern Russian border have gained their own independence.

II.

Belloc wrote a good deal about Islam. He had a grudging admiration for its persistence, for its historic military prowess, especially for its inconvertibility. In essence, he considered it a Christian heresy, with some similarities to Calvinism. Mohammed preached and insisted upon a whole group of ideas which were peculiar to the Catholic Church and distinguished it from the paganism which it had conquered in the Greek and Roman civilization.

Thus the very foundation of his teaching was that prime Catholic doctrine, the unity and omnipotence of god. The attributes of God he also took over in the main from Catholic doctrine: the personal nature, the all-goodness, the timelessness, the providence of God, His creative power as the origin of all things and the sustenance of all things by His power alone.[5]

Mohammed also maintained the existence of good and evil spirits, especially of Satan; he maintained the immortality of the soul "with the consequent doctrines of punishment and reward after death."[6] What began as a heresy became by practice and interpretation a separate religion, though still based on these original ideas.

If there is such agreement with the central core of Christian doctrine, what was the problem? Islam was an effort to simplify religion. What it rejected was the "complications" of Christian revelation. Mohammed "advanced a clear affirmation, full and complete, against the whole doctrine of an incarnate God. He taught that Our Lord was the greatest of all prophets, but still only a prophet: a man like other men. He eliminated the Trinity altogether."[7] The Trinity and the

Incarnation are, of course, the two basic Christian doctrines about the nature of God and His dwelling amongst us.

What followed from the denial of the Incarnation and the notion of "otherness" in the Godhead? The whole sacramental structure was gone—Mass, priesthood, and all that implied. This "simplification" is why Belloc found a similarity between Calvinism and Mohammedanism.

"Simplicity was the note of the whole affair; and since all heresies draw their strength from some true doctrine, Mohammedanism drew its strength from the true Catholic doctrines which it retained: the equality of men before God—'All true believers are brothers.' It zealously preached and throve on the paramount claims of justice, social and economic."[8] It might be noticed in retrospect that the reason the Taliban leaders in Afghanistan gave for refusing to turn over bin Laden when first demanded by the United States was the appeal to Muslim brotherhood.

In the current confrontation with Islam, not a few writers have stressed this "simplicity" theme to explain its relative attractiveness. Belloc's friend G. K. Chesterton had touched on what is at issue here in several places.[9] "A few centuries (after the Arian heresy) . . . the Church had to maintain the same Trinity, which is simply the logical side of love, against another appearance of the isolated and simplified deity in the religion of Islam," Chesterton wrote in *The Everlasting Man*.

> Yet there are some who cannot see what the Crusaders were fighting for; and some even who talk as if Christianity had never been anything but a form of what they called Hebraism coming in with the decay of Hellenism [Matthew Arnold]. Those people must certainly be very much puzzled by the war between the Crescent and the Cross. If Christianity had never been anything but a simple morality sweeping away polytheism, there is no reason why Christendom should not have been swept into Islam. The truth is that Islam itself was a barbaric reaction against that very humane complexity that is really a Christian character; that idea of balance in the deity, as of balance in the family, that makes that creed a sort of sanity, and that sanity the soul of civilization.[10]

What is at stake here is something much larger than might at first appear. For it is precisely this defense of "complexity" that makes the understanding of and use of the world possible. As Stanley Jaki has written, it is this notion of complexity, of creation and stable secondary causes that has made modern science possible and has, in its lack, caused Islam to fail to produce this same science.[11] Again one of the interesting aspects of the current war is the difference between sophisticated scientific warfare and terrorism carried on by relatively simple means.

III.

In addition to the theological side of Islam, which Belloc took with great seriousness, there was its military and cultural side. The First Chapter of his book, still a most exciting and, yes, sad book to read, begins: "Human affairs are decided through conflict of ideas, which often resolve themselves by conflict under arms."[12] Belloc understood where ultimate issues began and ended. Even though there were some four crusades launched against Islam in the Middle Ages, in Belloc's view, the only one that counted was the First (1095–99), though the most famous was probably the Third (1187–92). Belloc is quite clear that the Crusades were a defensive effort, a response to centuries of Islamic conquests at the expense of Christian lands and peoples.

The Crusades were aimed at recapturing Jerusalem and breaking the land connection between the Eastern and Western sectors of Islamic conquest. They almost succeeded but did not, in Belloc's view, because the Crusaders did not succeed in controlling all the land between the desert and the sea on the Eastern End of the Mediterranean. The final defeat by Saladin, a brilliant military genius, was at Hattin in Syria in 1187. The subsequent rise of the Ottoman Turks and their incursions into Europe are of interest to Belloc as a witness to the perennial nature of Islam to continue on what it calls its mission to conquer the world for Mohammed. The initial successes of Crusading armies established a feudal kingdom in Jerusalem. But it was the failure of the First Crusade, with its revelation of a lack of sufficient support from the European powers, that inaugurated it—France, the Empire, England— that spelled ultimate Islamic victory.

Belloc was clear that it made a difference who lost and who won wars. If this is classical realism, he was indeed a realist. "The military character of the opposing forces in these great duels of history means much more than the nature of their armament and of the personnel which waged the war on either side."[13] Belloc is aware of the geography, the character of the military commanders. He knows about chance, about incompetence. The Crusades sought to recover the old Roman Eastern and Southern conquests, but they failed. If there is one thing that overwhelms the reader of Belloc, it is the sense of a glorious effort that failed. This failure changed the very face of the modern world, which has very little understood the spiritual forces at work within it.

Today, Belloc's words of 1937 almost ring in our ears:

> That story (of Islamic victory) must not be neglected by any modern, who may think, in error, that the East has finally fallen before the West, that Islam is now enslaved—to our political and economic power at any rate if not to our philosophy. It is not so. Islam essentially survives, and Islam would not have survived had the Crusade made good its hold upon the essential point of Damascus. Islam survives. Its religion is intact; therefore its material strength may return. *Our* religion is in peril and who can be confident in the continued skill, let alone the continued obedience, of those who make and work our machines?[14]

We have here in a nutshell the essence of Belloc's thesis, one that occasions a further reflection on what this current war is about.

The secularism of the West is, no doubt, much more prevalent than in Belloc's time. The general view of this war is not one between "Christendom" and "Islam," but between "terrorists" and the secularized democracies. The solution of this problem, from the "terrorist" view point, is to conquer a decadent West. The alternate view is to get rid of the "terrorists" and allow to exist a form of rule in Islamic lands that conforms to modern notions of democracy, tolerance, and culture. This position can easily be looked upon as a new form of "colonialism" or even "imperialism" in which the solution to the military problem is to refashion the governments that are seen to be responsible for the problem in the first place.

There is a sense in which the current war can be seen as a struggle of secularist democracy against both a "fanatic" Islam and an equally "fanatic" Christianity, or at least what remains of it. All forms of religion, in this view, are seen to be "fanatical." It should not pass without note that, in the immediate aftermath of the WTC bombing, the initial response of the American people was in fact, in addition to being shocked, religious.

Belloc was quite conscious that the spiritual force of Islam has remained intact. He is amazed at its persistence and the sources of this strength. But he does not underplay it. He is quite clear that he thinks Islam will rise again. When it does, it will not find in the West a spiritual strength sufficient to counteract it. We might say, thus far, that since we still have men to "work the machines," Islam must remain relatively contained. And not all citizens in the West are in fact secularists.

If, however, modern secularist ideas could be imposed on Islam, especially those that deal with its population so that there would not be such a surplus of young men, then we could undermine its present attractiveness. Likewise, if we could invent something that would replace oil, say, a practical hydrogen-fueled motor, we could undermine the financial strength that had financed Islam's current power and ability to expand.

"There is with us a complete chaos in religious doctrine where religious doctrine is still held, and even in that part of the European population where the united doctrine and definitions of Catholicism survives, it survives as something to which the individual is attached rather than the community," Belloc concluded. "As nations we worship ourselves, we worship the nation; or we worship (some few of us) a particular economic arrangement believed to be the satisfaction of social justice. Those who direct us, and from whom the tone of our policy is taken, have no major spiritual interest."[15] Belloc's comment on "social justice" is itself extremely perceptive as many of those who blame America for all this wish to see the problem of Islamic aggressiveness to be one of its internal hurt feeling that it was being treated unjustly. Therefore, in this view, the problem was not Islam's but of the West. This sort of flawed analysis is quite prevalent in many modern religious analyses of ideological aggressiveness. It continually underestimates the vigor of spiritual forces. Islam, because of what it is, would be a problem without economics, without Israel, and without the modern world.

"Islam has not suffered this spiritual decline (found in the West)," Belloc affirms. Its spiritual power is seen everywhere within its own realms. "We are divided in the face of a Mohammedan world, divided by separate independent national rivalries, by the warring interests of possessors and dispossessed—and that division cannot be remedied because the cement which once held our civilisation together, the Christian cement, has crumbled."[16] Belloc is definitely not on the side of the "secularist" solution to the current problem of Islam. He sees the spiritual unity of the West has, in its absence, political consequences of the utmost importance.

One last point is worth making. It is often said that the current Mideast problem is largely caused by the presence of the Jews back on their ancient homeland, but a homeland that Islam now claims exclusively its own. This Jewish presence is supported by Western and currently American power. Belloc did not think that the problem of Islam was caused by the presence of a Jewish homeland under English sponsorship. He thought that the problem would be present even if no Jewish homeland ever existed. However, he did think that the presence of Jews in Palestine (he writes of course before the formation of an independent Jewish state) was an irritant.

> Of all the forms of foreign disturbance suffered by Syria in these new days of change, Zionism is the most violent and the most detested by the native population. That hatred may be called ineffective; the Jewish advance is bound to continue so long as there is peace and so long as the English are in undisputed possession. The Jews bring with them a much higher material civilisation, trained scientific experts, a largely increased exploitation of the land, and of all natural resources.[17]

But Belloc did not see the Jewish presence as merely a higher standard of living. The Jews too had their spiritual roots. They are "inspired by as strong a motive as can move men to action."

Yet, even with Jewish numbers increasing at the time, and standard of life, Belloc did not think it would ultimately be sufficient "against the fierce hostility of the Moslem world which surrounds them. That hostility is another moral force with which the future cannot but be filled. We in the West do not appreciate it because we do not hear its expression, we are not witnesses of the gestures nor partners in the conversations which fill the Near East; but if we ignore it we are ignoring something which may change our fate."[18] It is difficult to read these lines today without a sense of awe at their perceptiveness. Belloc's study of the Crusades, then, provides a unique and fascinating look at the relation of military and spiritual forces. To read him today is almost like reading current history, granted that he could not possibly have foreseen all the nuances of the present. Belloc was able to see "what might have been." He is left with the perplexity of Islam: what is it? Why does it remain?

Belloc makes us aware that, while we must study the side of Islam, and other religions we have something in common with, the fact remains that there is much that we do not have in common. This is recognized more clearly by Islam than by ourselves. Moreover, ideas, especially religious ideas, do have consequences. The answer to these ideas is not, as the secularists think, to get rid of any religion as a potential source of "fanaticism."

Rather some forum must be found in which the truth of the religions can be faced. This requires a politics and a military capable of making the conversations possible. Islam, Israel, and Christianity, the three religions of the Book, must recognize the dynamic consequences of their own relationship to one another. War may be necessary to make conversation possible, as Chesterton once remarked. What seems obvious in the aftermath of "terrorist" attacks is that God will not let the great religions leave the question of truth unresolved. Wars do not solve this prior problem. But the prior problem must be faced at its own level, that transcendent level wherein what counts, ultimately, is the truth of things.

Chapter 12

A CERTAIN LOSS

Belloc, in his essay "On a Lost Manuscript," in *On Nothing*, speaks whimsically of some pages that he lost in a cab, evidently a horse cab as he speaks of "a trap door on the top of the roof," on Vigo Street in London, "at the corner." He did not exactly lose his essay, but unaccountably left it in the cab. He even went to Scotland Yard to try to see if some honorable cabbie had turned it in, only to be told that "cabmen very rarely brought back . . . written things, but rather sticks, gloves, rings, purses, parcels, umbrellas, and the crushed hats of drunken men."

This lost essay was to have appeared on page 127 of *On Nothing* and was one that Belloc had worked upon until it was near perfect. He had kept it with him a whole year, rewriting, improving. It never left his side (he had no hard disc with a back-up). It crossed the Pyrenees seven times and the Mediterranean twice. Belloc even tells of fording the "Sousseyou," holding it high out of the water. Thus far, I have not been able to locate this river.

Belloc informs us of where he began to write this essay—". . . it was in Constantine, upon the Rock of Citra, where the storms came howling at you from Mount Atlas and where you feel yourself part of the sky." Oddly enough, I had written an essay (*Crisis*, November, 1996) about the seven Trappist monks from their Monastery in the same Atlas Mountains in Algeria, monks who were, on Easter, slaughtered by Muslim cadre.

And the only thing I vaguely recalled about Constantine was that I had some time ago read an essay of Albert Camus in which the city of Constantine appeared. I went to my shelves to see if I could find the reference. It turned out to be in an essay in Camus's *Lyrical and Critical Essays*, entitled, "A Short Guide to Towns without a Past."[1] I thought to myself both "What a wonderful title!" and "How could you have a *'long'* guide to towns without a past?"

This is what Camus said about Constantine, the place where Belloc wrote his lost essay, feeling himself "part of the sky": "In Constantine, you can always stroll around the bandstand. But since the sea is several hundred kilometers away, there is something in the people you meet there. In general, and because of this geographical location, Constantine offers fewer attractions, although the quality of its ennui is rather more delicate." One wonders what Belloc, that vital man, would have made of the notion of "delicate *ennui*"?

Belloc's lost manuscript was begun on the 17th of January in 1905. He was sitting where, as he unexpectedly recalled, the Numidian king Masinissa (210–149 B.C.) had come in "riding through the only gate of the city, sitting his horse without stirrups or bridle." Where is this from, I wonder—Livy? In any case, over his shoulder, an Arab was trying to read what Belloc was writing but could not understand the words; however, "the Muses understood and Apollo, which were its authors almost as much as I." Belloc was most pleased with his essay, the subject of which seems to have been the consequences to the Mediterranean coastal trade because of the opening of Suez, an unlikely subject for such lofty sentiments, to be sure, but with Belloc almost any topic sufficed to reach the highest things.

Belloc's essay is really, of course, about losing things, about the fact that as far as we know, things can indeed be lost. We are sometimes loathe to face this fact. He realized that he could never replace his essay; not even he could remember what he wrote or how he wrote it. He was aware of theories that would suggest that someday, in the future, beyond this life, perhaps, we could read this essay again, hear it praised for its worth—"I will not console myself with the uncertain guess that things perished are in some way recoverable beyond the stars. . . ."

This was not a skepticism about our destiny. Belloc, I think, must be understood in a way different from those of a more Platonic bent. He was too vividly aware of the loveliness of things and their passingness to be lightly put off by the prospects of future delight or knowledge. Thus, early in the essay, he writes, poignantly, "You all know how, coming eagerly to a house to see someone dearly loved, you find in their place on entering a sister or a friend who makes excuses for them. . . ." (On reading this touching sentence grammatically, it again brings to mind an exchange I once had about the English use of the apparently singular "someone" with the plural modifying pronoun "their.")

Clearly, Belloc does not end his essay in flaming hope. He does not maintain, however, that the possibility of seeing his essay again, possibly his loved ones again, is vain. He concludes, "It may be so. But the loss is certain."

Is this the "delicate ennui" that Camus experienced in Constantine suddenly appearing in Belloc? At first sight, it might seem so. But, as I said, this essay, the one not lost, is about losing things. Every day we see infinite things we shall never see again. Every day we compose essays in our minds we shall never write. We accustom ourselves, as we probably should, to notice mostly the things that might recur. We are not wrong to hope that "beyond the stars" we can recover what is lost.

But the first thing we must do is know that we have lost something. We must have enough love of reality, including the sticks, umbrellas, and the "crushed hats of drunken men," enough expectation "to come eagerly into a house" to know that someone is not there, something is lost. Only when we begin with this vivid realization of loss can we begin to hope. "It may be so. But the loss is certain."

As Belloc wrote on the Rock of Citra, in Constantine, "a town without a past," he recalled that the Numidian King Masinissa had ridden through the single gate of this city "sitting his horse without stirrups or bridle" —so it was, after all, a town with a history.

One of Belloc's essays is lost; not even Scotland Yard could find it. This loss is certain, because another of his essays, not on the "effect of the piercing of the Suez Canal upon coastwise trade in the Mediterranean," is not lost. I will not, in the end, say that "nothing was lost." I will say that the certainty that something is lost must be our beginning. "You all know how, coming eagerly to a house to see someone dearly loved, you find in their place on entering. . . ."

But the loss alone is certain.

63

Chapter 13

ON THINKING CONTINUALLY
OF THOSE IN BEATITUDE

In a letter from Manchester on August 13th, 1926, which I found in Robert Speaight's collection of Belloc's letters, Belloc wrote to Laura, Lady Lovat, that he had just been to a party with many friends.[1] His hostess, presumably Lady Lovat, was very kind and sent him a "parcel which contained a 1912 bottle of *Haut Brion*," which, as Belloc said, "astounded" him. I am not sure whether it was the *Haut Brion* itself that astounded him or the fact that Lady Lovat knew that he would like it, probably both. He was so inspired that he intended to complete his long poem on Wine that had been delayed for already four years. Belloc mused that "it will be a long time before I get Friendship and the Faith again under the same roof." Needless to say, these two belong together under the same roof, which is, more or less, the whole message of revelation.

Lady Lovat's daughter Rose died in August of 1940 at the age of fourteen. I do not know the exact circumstances of her death. As we know, Belloc's American wife, Elodie, died in 1914. He lost one son during World War I and another in World War II. He was privy to such sadness. Belloc wrote to Lady Lovat that he had been continually thinking of her daughter. He added:

> I have always believed that thinking continually of those in beatitude is a sign of communion with them. Of course, that may be a superstition, but it seems to me there must be something in it, for I have noticed that the degree in which the mind recalls those who are no longer on earth is connected with some sort of communion. I do not understand these things but I cannot help but feeling a

connection between actual persons and recurrent recollection. If it were not so why should one person be remembered more than another . . . .?

This is the Communion of the Saints, isn't it?

Belloc presumes to extend words of consolation, as only he can, to Lady Lovat. He wants to stress two things that, he writes, are results of his own experience. "The first thing is," he tells her, "that strong human ties escape the general rule of mortality." Belloc, of course, is most conscious of what he called in *The Path to Rome,* "the mortality of immortal men." Here he is telling us, apparently contrary to all evidence, that something escapes the "general rule of mortality." He realizes that this teaching goes against our culture and our senses. He does not pretend to explain it. "How that escape is accomplished, I have no idea. Most things pass, but certain forms of human affection do not pass; they seem to be of another stuff from the common fabric of life." In the face of doubt, including his own, he trusts his experience.

Notice how "scientific," if you will, Belloc is here. He does not have an a priori theory that prevents him from affirming his experience. He does not pretend to know how the experience comes about. On the other hand, he does not say that "since 'science' or philosophy tells us that there is no everlasting life, my experience of communion, even though I am aware of it, must be utter nonsense." What he knows, he admits; what he does not know, he also acknowledges.

The second thing that Belloc told Lady Lovat was that "human beings can rely permanently on doctrine." Here we see in Belloc a theme that we so often find in Chesterton, that the mind is a faculty of dogma, that its purpose is to state what is true. Since Belloc is here talking to a mother, his friend, about the death of her young daughter, it seems surprising that he is talking to her, of all things, about doctrine. We might be willing to accept vaguely that there is some affection that remains, but our mind should tell us that nothing remains.

Belloc admits to Lady Lovat that "doctrine is much drier than emotion and it is difficult to understand its full value today for the world has come today to depend wholly on emotion for its creed and its values." It seems remarkable that Belloc already saw, in 1940, a creed that has become commonplace at the end of the century. Remember that the doctrine at issue here is simply that of the Communion of Saints, the logical result of which would be that there is no reason why some communion between those of great mutual affection is not possible in theory. Belloc understands that this doctrine confirms his experience, which is what he is trying to explain to Lady Lovat.

Doctrine is, Belloc affirms, his "meat and drink." Then, almost in contradiction of what he has just said about his experience of communion, he explains the basic meaning of a doctrine that directly depends on faith: "I mean by doctrine that core of Catholic truth which is not to be referred to experience and not confirmed by experience—the doctrine of immortality is of this kind. The less vividly it is imagined, the more firmly it can be grasped." That is, if we try to imagine immortality, we will begin to confuse the principle at issue with our own imaginings, which may be quite far off base. Thus we can end up confused and doubtful not because of the doctrine but because of the imperfection of our imaginings.

Having said all of this, however, Belloc's conclusion to his letter to Lady Lovat is remarkable: "I am afraid that insisting on that truth (of immortality) is of very little value to anyone, because people can only live upon their feelings and doctrine itself is not alive."

Doctrine, no doubt, is alive as all thought is alive. We need to recall that immortality is both something that is believed in faith and also a philosophic conclusion, something discussed by Socrates on his last day. Christianity is not the source of the doctrine of individual immortality. That comes from Greek philosophy. Christianity arrives at immortality via the resurrection of the body, the problem of the continuity between the resurrected body and the soul separated from the same body at death.

So we must notice how good Belloc's advice to Lady Lovat, in her grief, really was. He told her of his own experience of communion, which he acknowledged to be a feeling or an emotion, but something real and to be reflected on none the less. He next suggested that there is a rather dry doctrine that might confirm this experience of communion if thought about, but that it was tough going for most people, though he thought it fitting to mention to Lady Lovat.

"I have always believed that thinking continually of those in beatitude is a sign of communion with them."

"The first thing is that strong human ties escape the general rules of mortality."

"Human beings can rely permanently on doctrine."

The doctrine on which we rely permanently confirms our thinking continually of our communion with those in beatitude. The persistent thinking of those in beatitude escapes the general rules of mortality. Faith and friendship are to be found under the same roof with immortality and the Communion of Saints, with, indeed, as Belloc would say in astonishment to Lady Lovat, "a 1912 bottle of *Haut Brion*!"

Chapter 14

ON REMEMBERING
"A REMAINING CHRISTMAS"

December requires a Christmas essay. In the back of my somewhat un-remembering mind, I recalled seeing an essay of Belloc's on Christmas. After looking through a number of Belloc books, I finally located his essay, "A Remaining Christmas," in the Penguin *Selected Essays*. Somehow, the date of this essay is not given in the list of acknowledgments that J. B. Morton gave about the essays' sources. I have not had time to check further, but that is not so important here when we deal with timeless things that happen in time.

After I began the essay, I realized, of course, that I had read this lovely essay before. In fact, the following title of the Chapter on Belloc in my *Another Sort of Learning* is taken from this essay—"The Immortality of Mortal Man." Indeed, this curious juxtaposition of mortality and immortality is what Belloc called a "shocking, and intolerable and, even in the fullest sense, abnormal thing." Christmas for Belloc was something that made this thoroughly wrenching situation of immortal beings who still die become somewhat "explicable, tolerable, and normal." How so?

"A Remaining Christmas" is about a man and his home. It is about a place wherein the things that change, and rapidly change, can find themselves confronted with things that do not change, with things *that are*. The very first sentence in Belloc's essay alerts us to our condition: "The world is changing very fast, and neither exactly for the better or the worse, but for division." The title of the essay, "A Remaining Christmas," gains its wording from the question that people ask, even more at the end of the century than in Belloc's time, "how much remains of the observance and of the feast and its customs?"

Belloc's essay is essentially an account of a single traditional Christmas. It takes place in an ancient house, the older parts of which date from the fourteenth century. It is a mile in the countryside. Off the central upper room of the house is "a chapel where Mass is said." The house is constructed of oak and brick. In the fireplace, only oak is burned.

In this large upper room is a huge oaken table which was originally built for an Oxford college, but looted from there by the Puritans. It was finally purchased from the family that inherited it from the Reformation. This table was made "while Shakespeare was still living, and the whole faith of England still hung in the balance; for one cannot say that England was certain to lose her Catholicism finally till the first quarter of that (17th) century was passed." The room was alight with candles, "the proper light for men's eyes," as Belloc rightly put it.

This is how Christmas Eve is spent in this house. On the morning of that Eve, large quantities of holly and laurel are collected from nearby trees and lots of the farm. Every room in the house is decorated with fresh smelling leaves, berries, needles, and boughs. A Christmas tree twice the size of a man is set up, to which little candles are affixed. Presents are there for all the children of the village, household members, and guests.

At five o'clock, already dark in England that time of year, the village children come into the house with the candles burning on the tree. There is first a common meal. Next the children come to the tree where each is given a silver coin and a present. Then the children dance and sing game songs. Belloc does not see this as quaint or accidental: "The tradition of Christmas here is what it should be everywhere, knit into the very stuff of the place; so that I fancy the little children, when they think of Bethlehem, see it in their minds as though it were in the winter depths of England, which is as it should be." The coming of Christ to Bethlehem is also His coming to the winter depths of England.

There is a Crib with animals, stars, shepherds, and the Holy Family. The children sing their carol at the Crib—"the one they know best begins, 'The First Good Joy that Mary had, it was the joy of One.'" I am sorry I do not know that carol. After the carols, all leave except the members of the household. The household dines, and, with the

Christmas fast, await Midnight Mass. The Yule log is carried in, so large that it takes two men to carry it. It is put on the great hearth. If it lasts all night and is still smouldering in the morning, this is supposed to be good fortune to the family. At Midnight, there is Mass and all take Communion.

All sleep late the next day to await the great Christmas dinner at midday. There is "turkey; and a plum pudding, with holly in it and everything conventional, and therefore satisfactory." The great feast lasts most of the rest of the day. Of the critics of these things, Belloc says, in an aside, that "they may reprove who will; but for my part I applaud." Then follow the twelve days of Christmas, ending with the Epiphany. All the greenery is to remain till this Day of the Magi, but by the end of that day, nothing is to remain. All the greenery is burned in a coppice reserved for these Christmas trees, "which have done their Christmas duty; and now, after so many years, you might almost call it a little forest, for each tree has lived, bearing witness to the holy vitality of unbroken ritual and inherited things." This unbroken ritual and the inherited things are our defense against meaningless change and our reminder that trees too are living vestiges of the work of God.

On New Year's, the custom was to open all the windows and doors of the house so, they say, that "the old year and its burdens can go out and leave everything new for hope and for the youth of the coming time." Some folks say this is superstition, but, Belloc pointed out, it is as old as Europe and goes back to forgotten times. At Midnight, all go outside to listen hushed for the arrival of the New Year. The people await the boom of a gun in a distant village to be sure that Midnight has arrived. The bells of the churches ring. When the bells cease, there is a silence. Then all go inside, the doors are shut, and all drink a glass.

Not merely death, but many things die and change all the time, and we can hardly bear this reality—"all the bitterness of living." And yet in this ritual, it all becomes "part of a large business which may lead to Beatitude." All these events of life are connected "holy day after holy day, year after year, binding the generations together."

In this house that celebrates what remains of Christmas, all the tragedies and joys of life have occurred within its rooms and halls. "But its Christmas binds it to its own past and promises its future; making the house an undying thing of which those subject to mortality within it are members, sharing in its continuous survival." The immortality of mortal men—Belloc sees in this ancient house with its tradition, with its yearly celebration of Christmas, a way to bear our lot, with the beloved things that change and pass. "There is this great quality in the unchanging practice of Holy Seasons, that it makes explicable, tolerable and normal what is otherwise a shocking and intolerable and even in the fullest sense, abnormal thing. I mean the mortality of immortal man."

Without these rituals of Christmas, their unchanging practice, we see that what is in fact shocking and intolerable and abnormal becomes inexplicable, becomes our lot and our culture. This is the nature of our times. We can no longer explain ourselves to ourselves. In failing to understand our immortality, we do not understand our mortality. And at Christmas, which we should see, as Belloc did, in our family tradition, such that Christ could also have come to the wintery depths of England, or to anywhere, we find in the Nativity the response to both our mortality and our immortality, in the Child with His parents, while the neighboring children sing the carol I do not know, "The First Good Joy that Mary had; it was the joy of One."

Chapter 15

ON BEING CLOSE TO THINGS PRIMARY

In the *Hills and the Sea*, Belloc tells of being high in the Pyrenees, in a place recalled as "Los Altos," which I cannot tell whether it is a specific area or merely that it is in a very high part of these very high mountains. The essay in which he tells us this is entitled "On 'Mails.'" He begins right away to tell us what "Mails" are. They turn out to be in fact "malls." Belloc describes a "mail" as a "place set with trees in regular order so as to form alleys, sand and gravel are laid on the earth beneath the trees, masonry of great solidity, grey, and exquisitely worked, surrounds the whole, except on one side, where strong stone pillars carry heavy chains across the entrance." The spelling "Mails" confused me.

Belloc did consistently put the term "mails" in quotation marks to indicate, I take it, an obsolete or foreign usage. I tried to find a dictionary or a reference book, a topic that shall come up shortly, to explain this usage. Finally, I found it in that microscopic version of the *Oxford English Dictionary*, after almost going blind with the magnifying glass. Evidently, it refers to a game, pall mall, or to a place where the game was played in Paris. I do not know this game, but the term Pall Mall is also a street in London where stylish folks once were said to live.

"Mails," Belloc tells us, take about two hundred years to perfect themselves and last in good condition for another hundred. They were popular during the time of Charles II of England and Scotland and Louis XIV in France. This essay is really about Belloc's "little pen" which has led him from one thing to another so much so that, at this point, he entirely forgets "The 'Mails'" until he realizes at the end of the essay that he has wandered into different intellectual and sentimental alleys.

At the mention of Louis XIV and Charles II, Belloc first begins to wonder which of these monarchs was older. He calculates this comparative age according to certain dates he does remember, the fact that Charles came back to England in 1660 and that Mazarin signed a Treaty with Spain in 1659. With such figuring, he finally decides that Charles is about thirty years older than Louis. At this point, of course, I eagerly wanted to look up the facts, which I did. It seems that Charles II was 1630–85, while Louis XIV lived from 1638–1715. So Belloc's memory was right on the money.

But this memory exercise was a literary trap for the reader, of course. Belloc himself could not look up the fact but had to recall it from his own memory because he was up in the Pyrenees at the time with no luxuries of civilization around him. "How dependent is mortal man on those Books of Reference," he sighs. At this point in my reading of this charming essay, I begin to wonder if I should have looked up the facts. Anyone with a few Books of Reference at his desk, Belloc observed, can seem more learned than Erasmus. There was the trap! Vanity! Belloc suggests in fact that "five out of six men who read this" essay will have such reference books at hand. I certainly did, which was why I could look up the dates and seem as wise as Erasmus.

But Belloc has another point to make, much more philosophical: "Let any man who reads this ask himself whether he would rather be where he is in London on this August day (for it is August), or where I am, which is up in Los Altos, the very high Pyrenees, very far from every sort of derivative and secondary thing and close to all the things primary?" This obviously rhetorical question—I know there are some dull souls who would still rather be in London even in August—forces us to ask ourselves about things secondary and things primary.

At this point, Belloc decides to describe what this rocky place in the high Pyrenees looks like. Beech and pine cling to the steep sides of the mountains, limestone precipices jut out. The going from camp site to camp site is very slow, dangerous. "It seems dead silent. There are few birds, and even at dawn one only hears a twittering here and there." The silence at first makes it seem as if nothing at all is being heard. Then he reflects that if he were suddenly to pick this Pyrenees place up and put it down in London, it would not be a silent place at all. What he hears at all times, day and night in Los Altos, is the roar of the torrent crashing down the steep mountainsides into the valley below. This noise has become so "continuous, so sedulous, that it has become part of oneself."

After several days, Belloc decides that he must begin to descend. Gradually, he notices signs of human life, an abandoned cabin, a path, "and thence to the high road and so to men." After he is among men for a while, he begins to think of where he has been. "I shall miss the torrent and feel ill at ease," he tells us, "hardly knowing what I miss, and I shall recall Los Altos, the high places, and remember nothing but their loneliness and silence" —a silence and loneliness that has become "part" of himself.

When he gets to the valley, Belloc will saunter into a town, "St. Girons or another, along the riverside and under the lime trees . . . ." And it was with this word "trees" that Belloc suddenly remembered "The 'Mails.'" the very topic about which he had begun to write. At this sudden ending, he addresses, with mock seriousness, his little fountain pen with which he is writing these reflections of his stay in the Los Altos, his "companion and friend." He asks it "whither have you led me, and why cannot you learn the plodding of your trade?" Of course, we are most grateful that this little pen did not learn the "plodding" of its trade. We are delighted that, with its user in charge, it rather wandered from place to place, from topic to topic, beyond the Books of Reference and the relative dates of Charles II and Louis XIV, but, all the while, still remembering in mountains and, yes, in the "Mails" that take two hundred years to mature, "nothing but loneliness and silence." Here at last, we are again reminded to distinguish in our lives the things of "secondary" and "primary" importance, the great task of our existence.

Part 4

"What landscape was to Milton, what urban eccentricity was to Dickens, what the mathematic was to Pascal, that the personality of Samuel Johnson was to James Boswell. It fed, it invigorated, it moulded, it provided full purpose. The chances are that no one else could have played Johnson's part, and very probably, almost certainly, no one else could have played Boswell's part in the arrangement. Whereon hangs an interesting side issue: 'What are the chances, one in how many million, of such a juxtaposition?' I cannot answer that question, nor can anybody else; but we can at least say that the odds are so heavy that 'chance' is the wrong word, and some more old fashioned title such as Providence, the right one."

—Hilaire Belloc, "Boswell," *The Silence of the Sea*, 1940.

Chapter 16

ON TOWNS AND PLACES

"There is a river called the Eure which runs between low hills often wooded, with a flat meadow floor in between. It so runs for many miles. The towns that are set upon it are for the most part small and rare, and though the river is well known by name, and though one of the chief cathedrals of Europe stands near its source, for the most part it is not visited by strangers."

— Hilaire Belloc, "Home."[1]

I.

In a few lines, Belloc memorably tells us of a river in northern France, the Eure, one, as we look it up, that flows into the Seine above Rouen at Pont d'Arche. It has towns along it, none very famous. It is 140 miles long. Near its headwaters, the famous cathedral of Chartres is located. It is indeed "one of the chief cathedrals of Europe," of the world. It is a place that all know or would like to know. But strangers do not much visit the river itself. Obviously, Belloc has been there, probably walked its banks, if not rowed or sailed on it.

Belloc informs us that he was once in this river valley, while, in fact, "drawing a picture of the woods." Here he ran into an Englishman who was, as he put it, "in the oddest way." By the looks of him, bent knees and leaning forward, he did not seem to care about how far he had yet to go. Belloc looked at him. "He was in the clothes of an English tourist," he tells us, "which looked odd in such a place." Then, on second thought, Belloc added, "as, for that matter, they do anywhere." What was it Chesterton said was the mark of the travelling Englishman? "When in Rome do exactly as you did at home."

We cannot but be amused at the scene in northern France, an out-of-place Englishman in travel togs, meeting the half-French Belloc who is sketching the woods along the Eure. Did Belloc himself, we wonder, dress like an "odd" English tourist? We doubt it, though we know he tramped over most of Europe, the near-East, America, and northern Africa. While on his *Path to Rome*, I believe that he vowed not to change his boots until he reached the Eternal City. As I recall, they were worn out long before he got there for High Mass on the Feast of Sts. Peter and Paul. Actually, though he got to Rome in time, he missed High Mass, having first settled into a nearby trattoria. But, as he assures us, he kept the letter of the vow.

I shan't go on with this story, whose very title, if we know Belloc, is the essence of what existence is all about, the real "home" of man, the relation of this home to his eternal home. But this essay of but ten pages for me captures the almost mesmerizing way that Belloc draws us into another world, a world that he had actually seen and described.

At the beginning of *The Four Men*, Belloc told us that we must hasten to capture our time and place, the time and place in which we actually live, lest they be forever lost. If we do not so capture them, they will not come again. Already here we have the later-famous theme of "You can't go home again," a principle that, as far as I can tell, never stopped anyone from trying, if only in his memory.

A man remains content in his love for his own county. The man called "Myself" tells us of this contentment in *The Four Men*. But he, nonetheless, senses an approaching "doom."

> Then, believe me, Sussex, he is anxious in a very different way; he would, if he could, preserve his land in the flesh; and keep it here as it is, forever. But since he knows he cannot do that, "at least," he says, "I will keep here its image, and that shall remain." And as a man will paint with a peculiar passion a face which he is only permitted to see for a little time, so will one passionately see down one's own horizon and one's fields before they are forgotten and have become a different thing.[2]

We can preserve neither the Eure, along which we drew the woods, nor Sussex, our native county, against the doom to which all things human are subject. We are permitted to see things—faces, fields, cathedrals, woods, and rivers—for such a little time. The fields and the houses we knew will be forgotten unless we sketch them, write of them, or remember them as they were when we first saw them.

II.

A friend of mine travels to London Town not infrequently. Once he asked me if I needed anything from London. I asked him to find for me a book of Belloc. He did. It was called *Places*. It was published in 1942. I had never read it before, never heard of it, such is Belloc's prolificness.

Sometime later, my friend came back again from London with another book. This time it was *Towns of Destiny*, a handsome book of 1927. This book contains, as many of Belloc's books do, his own sketches, though the sketches in *Towns of Destiny* are by Edmund Warre. And they are very fine. The sketches in *The Path to Rome* and in *The Four Men* are those by Belloc himself. I have often contemplated them.

Places begins with the following intriguing question: "It is a nice question whether ignorance or stupidity play the greater part in human affairs."[3] This "ignorance or stupidity" dichotomy seems to be a complete disjunction. Belloc has little patience with politicians, particularly those involved in "foreign affairs." In his Introduction, he wishes that people in England would know "more about other people." How much we can know of anyone, of course, is limited by time, insight, freedom, and good will.

Usually the great bond of people is "religion," he thought, "but of that bond people today know nothing." One wonders what Belloc would have thought of the statistics about religion in England in our time!

Thus, a "secondary and much feebler bond is travel."[4] Yet, of the usefulness of travel, Belloc is not confident. "I am afraid," he tells us, "I do not believe very much in the effect of travel as an aid to wisdom unless it be accompanied by a profoundly transcendental and a universal philosophy." But this philosophy is no longer available to us. We are thus like boulders rolling down the hill on "a blind course." What we see may be only a "ruin." He adds that "with these profound and pleasing thoughts, I leave you."

Then echoing what he told us in T*he Four Men*, he concludes his Introduction: "I have here collected many an impression of travel of the sort which I fear can never be repeated in a ruined world." And what places does he see in this ruined world? Among other places, he is in Stockholm, Danzig, Cracow, Moscow, Falaise, Avignon, Luxembourg, St Peter's in Rome, Lisbon, then Burgos, Patmos, Carthage, Aleppo, Damascus, Nazareth, and Capharnaum.

And *Places* ends with an essay, appropriately enough, yet unexpected too, called, "About Wine." In this latter essay, Belloc writes, "There is no wine, I am told, in China, nor among the Hindoos; nor any among the peoples of the Pacific, unless you count the Australians, who have, as we all know, planted vineyards and rigorously taken to wine-making. Wine is a part of the soul of Europe and proper to ourselves. When we find it in far-off places, the Cape or California, it is but a colony of ourselves."[5]

Wine, moreover, has theological overtones. "For who can be properly nourished, if indeed he be of human stock, without wine? St. Paul said to someone who had consulted him (without remembering that, unlike St. Luke, he was no physician), 'Take a little wine for your stomach's sake.' But I say take plenty of it for the sake of your soul and all that appertains to the soul: scholarship, verse, social memory and the continuity of all culture."[6] He hints that, God bless him, St. Paul practiced medicine without a license, but his medical prescriptions were rather sparing in their understanding of civilization and the fluid that energizes it.

Wine is not primarily a medicine of the body but of the soul. And notice the things of souls that Belloc lists that flow from it: scholarship, verse, social memory, and the continuity of all culture. That is an interesting list indeed, particularly the last item. Contrary to what we might expect, wine does not darken the memory but serves the very "continuity of culture" itself.

But dark memories are found in Belloc. He tells us, in *Places*, that he has written of Stockholm before. Between visits to that town, his memory of it changed. "When I first saw it, it seemed to me more beautiful than it did when I saw it the second time. But I daresay the change was in myself and not in Stockholm," Belloc tells us.[7] New modern buildings had been erected, but he acknowledges differences in taste. "What I have in common to all my memories of Stockholm is the dignity and ubiquity of the calm Swedish water which gives its note to all that land."[8] It is a land of lakes and "miles of repeated trees." Stockholm is credited with more history "than any other of the lesser capitals in Europe." The reason for this was that its sixteenth-century kings were also warriors.

Stockholm calls itself the "Venice of the North." But Belloc, aside from the water, sees very little similarity between these two cities. "Venice is queenly, Stockholm is homely." Venice is a city of wealth. It is wrong to think that wealth in a city is everything. "But when it (wealth) has been present it should be remembered, for wealth (as the philosopher said—and he delighted, as you know, in the obvious and commonplace) purchases many things."[9] But there is more to Venice than wealth. "There was some spirit or other which gloried through it all and now still shines with an undying flame."[10]

Stockholm's beauty comes from "without," as Belloc saw it. "As your ship moves away from Venice, you look back on a distant vision of splendour, man-made and a triumph for a man. As your ship moves away from Stockholm, you look back upon something grey which mixes with undistinguished hills around." The contrast gets at two different things within the human spirit. The one is the splendor of man, the other of this earth.

Belloc continued: "Nevertheless, Stockholm contains this secret of the north, *mystery.*" It is a place of "legends and episodes which touch on things beyond the world—but things of the night: winter things." In retrospect, in reading such lines, one cannot help but think of the aura around the films of Ingmar Bergman. Sweden, of course, is known as a worldly place, a place of the future of natural man. Yet, there are the Norse and Scandinavian tales.

Belloc ends his account of Stockholm with a reference to General Axel von Fersen, who was a lover of Marie Antoinette. Years later, von Fersen was murdered by a mob. But "his mind was furnished with nothing but one great memory of a poignant ineradicable sort, which belonged to his youth." He had helped the French Queen, husband, and children escape to Varennes. There is a story, perhaps "only a myth," that in his killing, von Fersen's severed hand is put in a boat where it takes on a strange light that guides the way. Was it true? "It is in tune with those visions of things beyond the world and things not of the holier sort with which stories of those woods, those streams, those hills are full."[11]

The next stop of Belloc that I wish to narrate is perhaps of a different spirit than the "mystery" that we find in Scandinavia. This is Patmos, the island off of Turkey on which John the Evangelist died. He is the writer of the Apocalypse, so he is connected with the mood of Belloc's reflections on Stockholm.

Belloc, himself a sailor, came into Patmos by boat. He saw on a summit the Monastery of St. John. The diversity of the Aegean Islands makes the sea more wondrous. But what strikes the westerner is the "barrenness of the land." The land is fertile. It would "bear dense growth and nourish large trees, as in antiquity they did. What has destroyed the forests has been the Mohammedan blight."[12] Belloc reports what he sees. "Islam is the enemy of the tree, as it is the enemy of all patient and continuous human effort." When St. John saw this Island it was not so. The relationship of theology and economics is closer than we admit.

Both trees and houses are lacking on Patmos. "If we could get a full picture of what all that sea-world was in the early Christian time and compare it with what we see today we should understand what ruin false doctrine can bring upon the world."[13] The "ruin" caused by false doctrines is almost a forbidden topic. St. John, Belloc tells us, was "exiled" to this island long before the Muslim era. Belloc wonders why John was exiled to this tiny island. The modern city is filled with various police, whatever they are called. Antiquity was not so sophisticated.

Belloc sees a different problem from Islam in the earlier time of John. What was the relation between the Church and "the ancient civilization?" It was in this ancient civilization that the Church began and ultimately flourished. Benedict XVI pointed out that Christianity first faced this civilization of the philosophers. St. John was an example of the difference between these two civilizations, Christianity and the classical civilization. How do they fit together?

"We know very well why the virulent, debased, modern hostility to the Faith is what it is. It is the hatred of corruption for health, the hatred of vice for virtue. But why should that which made the height of loveliness in verse and in stone have wrestled with complete beauty, and attempted to destroy the only final harmony?"[14] This is the most intriguing of questions.

"The Catholic Church did not come to destroy but to complete." Belloc wrote. "Unfortunately, that which it came to complete was too well satisfied with its own evil as well as with its own good." This situation left it unable to understand the new in the light of the old. "There is about the Catholic Church something absolute which demands, provokes, necessitates alliance or hostility, friendship or enmity. That truth you find unchangeable throughout the ages, and therefore it is, that, on the first appearance of the church, the challenge is already declared— and that is what is meant by Patmos."

St. John is particularly singled out by the enemies of religion. And this enmity is not just ancient. "It is, and has been, much more the modern anti-Christian attack which is and has been obsessed by him."[15] This obsession is primarily because John is the theologian of the Incarnation, which means that one within the Trinity, the Godhead, became man, true God and true man.

III.

Towns of Destiny was published in 1927. Belloc narrates visits to some thirty towns that he has visited in Spain, Portugal, France, Germany, North Africa, and Italy. Among others, we find Segovia, Oporto, Constantine, Carthage, Le Mans, Metz, Worms, and Narbonne. His first section is about Spain, the first chapter of which is entitled, "The Entry into Spain."

These are his first words in the book: "Of all the provinces of Christendom, Spain possesses most intensely that kind of unity and personality which come from a defined boundary. Things only are because they are one, and a city is most a city when it is sharply defined by a wall."[16] We Americans have always lived in un-walled cities. Belloc makes us wonder if we have missed something.

I want to comment on two of the cities that Belloc wrote of in

Towns of Destiny, Cefalù in Sicily and Corneto in Italy. All Belloc's towns had their own "destiny" in which they came to the fore in one time or another. Cefalù was known to Richard of England. It was once controlled by the Saracens. Corneto was the town of the Tarquins, sixty miles north of Rome on the sea.

"On the Northern shore of Sicily, well westward of its midmost point, stands a rock and a town which may be taken for the type of the re-conquered lands. These are the rock and town of Cefalù."[17] The re-conquered lands are those which are re-conquered from the Saracens, the claim to which their descendants have never relinquished.

Cefalù, with its massive rock rising a thousand feet, was first a fortress, but the town arose below it in the peace of Roman rule. Like Palermo, it was a much captured town. "Greece gave it its headland name. Carthage ruled it: Rome wrested it away. In the height of the Dark Ages—perhaps before the death of Charlemagne—Islam had planted a garrison here and made it an outpost of that sweeping of the Mediterranean whereby the Mohammedan and his Asia so nearly overwhelmed us."[18] Then the first of the Normans arrived with Roger of Sicily. As a result of a vow, Roger built the great Norman cathedral there, with its mosaics, a combination of Byzantium and early Gothic. It is still there.

After the destruction caused by Islam, the Normans restored order to Sicily. It is the cathedral that fascinates Belloc. He describes the apse of the cathedral in Cefalù: "The great subject is Christ in Judgment, the Heroic Face that dominates all the nave from above. He holds in His right hand the Open Book of Record, His left is raised for acquittal or sentence." This is the very theme found in Benedict's great Encyclical, *Spe Salvi*, the Judgment of the living and the dead. This Head of Christ in the nave had "looked down upon Christian men for more than seven centuries." Then Belloc adds, "May the evils of a coming time spare it!"

There is something more about this nave. Around it are inscribed "the noblest motto yet found for the Judge and Redeemer and Brother of mankind."[19] This very motto, as Belloc tells us, was what inspired the famous painting of (John Singer) Sargent found in the Boston Public Library, which Belloc had also once evidently visited. Sargent's painting shows the "Fall of the Old Gods." Rising in the center of this scene is the Crucifixion, as what replaced them.

The motto in Cefalù reads as follows: "*Factus homo factor hominis factique redemptor / Judico corporeus corpora corda Deus.*" Belloc renders the Latin into English as follows: "I, having been made man, and being the Maker of Man, and the Redeemer of what I made, judge in bodily form the bodies and the hearts of man: for I am God."[20]

In the painting of Sargent, one word of the Latin text was changed. Christ in the painting was not "Christ in Judgment but Christ crucified." Thus the word "*judico*" was changed to "*Redimo.*" In the painting in the Boston Library, the motto read: "*Factus homo factor hominis factique redemptor / Corporeus redimo corpora corda Deus.*" It would thus read: "I, having been made man, and being the Maker of Man, and the Redeemer of what I made, redeem in bodily form the bodies and the hearts of man: for I am God." Belloc adds: "I think his (Sargent's) genius to discover, and to be inspired by, such lines was as great as that which produced his painting."

Belloc was most struck by this rock on the north shores of Sicily with the town's cathedral. He is reminded of the North, "of Lisieux or Coutances," but also, in the mosaics, of the Bosporus.

> It was strange, under the eyes of such a Face as that which looked down upon us from the eastern roof, to see a baptismal font supported by the fierce leopards of the Dark Ages, the mythology of Anjou and Maine, the things men imagined during the long wars against the heathen of the North Sea, before Europe awoke to the noisy splendour of the Crusades.[21]

There is something prophetic in these lines, the wars with the heathen in the North, the belated waking up of what moves from the South.

The last essay in *Towns of Destiny* is "Corneto, of the Tarquins." This is the old Etruscan town north of Civitavecchia. It too in the early middle ages was destroyed by the Saracens. But it is at the origins of the Roman religious rites. Not much is known of the Etruscans—"the Etrurian people and through them the iron laws, the subterranean vision of death, the dusk of religion, which they imposed on Rome and from which we all inherit."[22]

Belloc is struck by the tombs he finds in the area. "I did not descend among them, among those dead. I did no more than walk out through the early evening into their vast, deserted field. I came back before the end of the day to look at the great stone coffins which have been gathered in the museum of the town."

The stone faces of the coffins impressed Belloc. He saw the carved head of a young man "on the point of waking" but in repose. There was a sense of the soul being hunted here, of its immortality. It is this "doctrine of immortality which has made Europe the head of the world."[23] Why so? we wonder. But this doctrine was already with the Egyptians and the Etruscans, where it was still "confused, without dogma." Undefined dogmas are dangerous.

Belloc noticed the tomb of a matron, who must have been buried there, for "never have I seen any stone living more intensely with personality." He describes her. "There was no pretense to beauty, nor even to a beauty lost in that face of middle age, but a singular majesty and a full bearing of that burden which we, the Christians, in our later age, call also the duty of living." "Who was she?" Belloc wonders. "Of what sons was she the mother? Of what soldier the widow, or of what lord? What fields were the fortune of the great family from whom she inherited?"[24]

We can wonder about such things even of an ancient Etruscan woman. "If ever there was a face made for ever, it is that face. I shall come back to it again. For Corneto, once seen, is a place to which a man returns as he returns to the Capitol or to his home." This again is the theme of Belloc that we saw in the beginning, the return to our home. We find here in Corneto the memory, in stone, of a people "wholly preoccupied with the great business not only of life, but of death."

What did the artist who carved this face have in mind? The normal things, "the bearing of children; the governance of a household; the loss of this and that affection and companionship; and all, whatever losses beside, make up the burden of mankind. Therein also was the last descent out of the light of the sun; the last and mortal loss of all." One cannot help but notice in that passage that abiding concern of Belloc which perhaps bothered him more than any other, as he tells us in *The Path to Rome*. This is the loss of companionship that we shall never have again, at least in this world.

"When I had left my long contemplation of that Face I went up upon the ramparts of the city and looked down over the sea." We know not from whence life came. This image of life coming and going is the lesson of Corneto. There is no hint here of where these stones and tombs came from. For many, life itself is like that.

Belloc concludes the *Towns of Destiny* with ancient, tiny Corneto, not with Munich, or Edinburgh, or Lyons. "This place, how many thousands pass in a week along the main line that runs below Corneto from the north: from Leghorn, from Genoa, from the slime of the Riviera, from Paris, from London, all on their way to the hotels of Rome. And how many know what they are passing? *They are passing the things of life and death.*"[25]

If Belloc has anything to teach us in the places and towns of this world, it is this admonition "not to pass the things of life and death."

"A man will paint with a peculiar passion a face which he is permitted to see for but a little time."

"He was in the clothes of an English tourist, which looked odd in such a place, as, for that matter, they do anywhere."

"It is a nice question whether ignorance or stupidity play the greater part in human affairs."

"For who can be properly nourished, if indeed he be of human stock, without wine?"

"Nevertheless, Stockholm contains this secret of the north, *mystery.*"

"That burden which we, the Christians, in a later age, also call the burden of living."

"We should understand what ruin false doctrine can bring upon the world."

"There is about the Catholic Church something absolute which demands, provokes, necessitates alliance or hostility, friendship or enmity."

"I, having been made man, and being the Maker of Man, and the Redeemer of what I made, judge in bodily form the bodies and hearts of men: For I am God."

"Factus homo factor hominis factique redemptor / Corporea redimo corpora corda Deus."

Chapter 17

THE FIGHT FOR GOOD THINGS

Included in the Dorothy Collins collection of Chesterton essays (Methuen, 1949) is an essay on Belloc. This essay was originally found in a volume entitled *G.K.C. as M.C.*, from the year 1929. It is obviously an occasion on which Chesterton introduced Belloc to some audience. I cannot find my copy of *G.K.C. as M.C.*

Obviously, the audience knows both Chesterton and Belloc. Chesterton begins with the famous line, "When I first met Belloc he remarked to the friend who introduced us that he was in low spirits." To this Chesterton adds, after coming to know him, that Belloc's low spirits were "much more uproarious and enlivening than anybody else's high spirits." One wonders how Belloc's "high spirits" would have been described! I love the adjectives "uproarious" and "enlivening."

In many ways, Belloc often seemed like a sad man. I have often thought that it had to do with a realization that the final place for our "high spirits" is not in this world, a world that Belloc loved so much and described so well on his walks. The words near the end of the *Path to Rome* have always haunted me: "Human companionship once broken can never be restored, and you and I shall not meet or understand each other again. It is so of all the poor links whereby we try to bridge the impassable gulf between soul and soul." No passage in our language brings us closer to the wonderment about everlastingness than that of this breaking of human companionship.

Chesterton recalled that, on the evening of their first meeting, they talked long into the night. Belloc left behind "a glowing track of good things." After recording this marvelous comment about his friend, Chesterton thought it well to explain what he meant. His words were not just talk, *"bons mots."* Rather, when he spoke of "good things," he meant it quite literally. Belloc, he said, "has made the greatest fight for good things of all the men of my time."

We might reflect on that statement. We would not find it said in any modern history book that it was precisely Belloc who put up the greatest fight "for good things" in his time. The issue, of course, is what we mean by "good things," the definition of which is, after all, what modern times are about. The battles of the world are really over what we mean by good things. We cannot forget that it is in the capacity of men and nations to define and put into effect bad things, which they then call "good things." This confusion may well be the intellectual content of our times, which Belloc saw from the beginning.

Chesterton said that he had his own "hobby of the romance of small things, including small commonwealths." We still see the war with modernity in Europe. It tries to decide whether to become a 'modern state,' which stands over and above its diverse people, at least over those who survive Europe's population decline. In that context, it seems amazing that Belloc was the one, who, almost eighty years ago, saw that Islam would rise again and why.

Later on in his introduction, Chesterton says of Belloc: "What he brought into our dream was this Roman appetite for reality and for reason in action, and when he came into the door there entered with him the smell of danger." That is a curious combination: reality, reason in action (prudence), and danger. Reason really is dangerous in a society that rejects truth and the direction of reason itself.

To describe the complexity of Belloc's character, Chesterton writes: "It was no small part of the irony in the man that different things strove against each other in him, and these not merely in the common human sense of good against evil, but one good thing against another." We often think that our main struggles are against good and evil. Many no doubt are, yet, the more poignant ones are between good and good, between a religious vocation and marriage, between working for the poor and working for the rich, between serving one's country and serving one's school.

As I often say, Belloc is the greatest essayist in the language. He also writes so wonderfully about places and towns and people. Chesterton catches this: "I have not spoken of those glorious and fantastic guide books which are, as it were, the text-books of a whole science of Erratics. In these he is borne beyond the world with those poets whom Keats conceived as supping at a celestial 'Mermaid.'" Here is Chesterton's own "Great Inn at the End of the World." It is Belloc's companionship and its breaking.

I was curious about Chesterton's use of the term of Belloc that his works comprised the "whole science of Erratics." The word erratic is generally pejorative. It means inconstant, inconsistent. But the earlier meaning of the word means rather nomadic, something moving around. And that is Belloc. He walked to see the world, and he saw it. Indeed, the world he saw is only preserved in what he wrote. We did not know how to keep it otherwise.

In the end though, Belloc is indeed "borne beyond the world with those poets conceived . . . as supping at a celestial 'Mermaid.'" Yes, I think, both Belloc and Chesterton are waiting for us to sup at a celestial Mermaid tavern and, to recall the end of *Dickens*, to drink the great flagons in the "Inn at the End of the World."

Chapter 18
ON IRONY AS THE "AVENGER OF TRUTH"

Irony is a flourishing topic of study today in many academic circles. Indeed, academia itself is one of the prime subjects for irony. No one today, for instance, would simply accept without amusement the notion that the academy is where you find unvarnished truth in our society. Almost everyone has heard of the rigid closure to truth that is found throughout the universities. The title of Allan Bloom's now famous, but hardly attended to, book, *The Closing of the American Mind,* is ironical, as befits a good student of Plato. It is simply amusing and bittersweet that a book on the status of the intellectually open university would portray its mind as precisely "closed."

In the *Selected Essays* (Penguin) of Belloc, we find an essay, "On Irony." It is a remarkable essay. Indeed it is the justification of irony as a legitimate but dangerous tool in the pursuit of truth itself. We sometimes have to speak the truth over the heads of someone who will not listen, but it is not irony unless there is some third party, even if it is God, who does listen to the implied, hence ironical, truth.

Take for instance that passage from the Declaration of Independence about self-evident truths among which is that all men have a right to life. Our judges, politicians, and reporters may well cite this passage with great solemnity as if this obvious principle is one quite widely accepted in our society. The very reciting of the passage is ironical in a society where millions are legally killed and the lives of many others constantly in jeopardy. A Pope will say, on the contrary, that we live in a culture of death. He speaks no irony, though the culture will not admit it to itself.

"It is the intention of irony," Belloc tells us, "that it should do good, because it is of the nature of irony that it should avenge the truth." How does it do this avenging? Irony intends to inflict a wound. It points out to someone, anyone, the breach not only between what we say and what we do, but between what we do and what is right. Irony cannot be used with any "propriety except in God's service."

Thus Belloc thinks that if we are morally compromised, we will not see ourselves as we are. We will have no criterion against which to see our depths. "The history of Letters is full of men who, tempted by this or that, by money or by ease, or by random friendship, or by some appetite lower than the hunger and thirst after justice, have found their old strong irony grow limp and fruitless after they had sold their souls." What a remarkably powerful sentence that is—limp and fruitless men who have sold their souls!

Irony seems to be for men of the world. It is a strange virtue, if virtue it is. "To the young, the pure, and the ingenuous, irony must always appear to have in it a quality of something evil, and so it has, for . . . it is a sword to wound. It is so directly the product or reflex of evil that, though it can never be used—nay, can hardly exist—save in the chastisement of evil, yet irony always carries with it some reflections of the bad spirit against which it was directed." The "ironical man"— Socrates was said to be such—was often seen by his listeners to be mean-spirited or merely jesting with them. They did not grasp the truth he was indicating.

Belloc understands irony to be a primary weapon to "defend right against wrong." Indeed, the "bad spirit" that irony seems to take over from the evil it attacks would suggest that we should not use it. Yet, Belloc says, "how false it is to say that vengeance and the hatred of the evil men are in themselves evil, all human history can prove." Vengeance, the requiting of an evil in the name of justice, the hatred of evil men, that is, the hatred of what they do, is not itself evil.

Belloc appeals to the common sense and practice of mankind as witness. A society or people that bear absolutely no anger at evil done to the good or innocent, that has nothing but praise for the evil that men do, is itself a corrupt society that can feel nothing of the divine wrath, nothing of the divine criterion of right and good.

This is heady doctrine, Belloc knows. "A happy world, such as the world of children, or any society of men who have still preserved the general health of the soul—such a society may be found in many moun-tain valleys—needs none of this salt for the curing and the preservation of morals." Yet, most societies are filled with the evil that occasions irony, from the poets and the old men who have known some wisdom.

But, perhaps too close to home, what about a generally corrupt society, one that enacts the violations of the commandments as its good deeds, as its rights? "There is a last use for irony, or rather a last aspect of it, which this general irony of nature and nature's God suggests: I mean that irony which can only appeal in the letters of a country where corruption has gone so far that the mere truth is vivid with ironical power." We can live in a society in which even the statement of the Commandments is ironical, since their very statement speaks against what is going on everywhere.

Belloc did not live a happy life in many ways. But he did great good to his fellows and secured a "singular advantage to his own soul" because the evil in things was not allowed to pass unspoken. "How false it is to say that vengeance and the hatred of evil men are in themselves evil." What Belloc added to the normal wounds that irony is intended to inflict on evil doings is wit and laughter, the two things the mind in moral and intellectual error can least stand to hear directed to itself.

Belloc concludes with a penetrating sentence: "No man possessed of irony and using it has lived happily; nor has any man possessing and using it died without having done great good to his fellows and secured a singular advantage to his own soul." No doubt there is something autobiographical in these powerful lines of Belloc. He did not suffer fools lightly, but he did enjoy them. He hated evil and was not afraid to call it such, even when he had to speak ironically about it, even when, even today, when we read him, we see that he speaks to God when he refuses to call evil anything other than it is.

Chapter 19

BELLOC'S MRS. MARKHAM
ON THE AMERICANS

In 1986, Loyola University of Chicago Press published *GK's Weekly: A Sampler*. This volume collected thirty sundry reprints of *GK's Weekly*, from the first one of March 21, 1925 to the one, dated June 18, 1936, following Chesterton's death. Evidently, a total of 588 issues of *GK's Weekly* were published. Each issue was full of the seriousness, spoof, irony, sanity, information, philosophy, and wit that we associate with Chesterton and his friends.

Along the way, Belloc had a series featuring a mother, Mrs. Markham, who would "explain" the facts of life, political and otherwise, to her two very precious and pert children, Tommy and Mary. In some anthology I once read, this same Mrs. Markham explained "policemen" to her offspring. I remember reading it on the local "Metro" (underground). I cried because it was so funny. So I was pleased to notice several of these "Mrs. Markham teachings" in *GK's Sampler*—explanations of "lawyers," "newspapers," and "the history of England."

Mary frequently wants Mamma to explain "Kangaroos." But Mamma thinks that explaining the police is a more useful enterprise "because people who make mistakes about Policemen suffer terribly in later life." The children seem to be about nine or ten, both blessed with acid tongues, plus wit far beyond their years. They are always ironically grateful to their mother for setting them straight about what goes on in life.

The satiric flavor of these wonderful "teachings" can be garnered from Mrs. Markham's explanation of "Americans" (June 23, 1928—written about five months after Schall is born in Iowa, USA). Mary asks, since they now know of elephants, if Mamma will not "speak of Americans." Tommy is likewise enthusiastic, "Yes, Mamma, you promised me to talk about these fascinating beings." The idea that Americans might be, in the eyes of her children, "fascinating beings" was a bit much for Mrs. Markham. She suspects her son of untoward insinuations. "The phrase 'fascinating beings,'" she continues, "seems to me, my dear Tommy, inappropriate, and (*looking at him severely*) I am not quite sure that your intention. . . ."

Tommy is up to his mother's level; he is in fact "eager." "I assure you, dear Mamma, the words were used in a flattering sense, and my eagerness for information perhaps outstripped my discretion." One is never quite sure if little Tommy is a budding genius or an inchoate monster, probably both.

Mrs. Markham accepts this explanation cautiously but adds: "Well then, I must first inform you that the Americans are our cousins. . . ." At this point we realize that Mrs. Markham has already instructed her own logical children on other topics. Thus, young Miss Mary interrupts the conversation: "You told us that long ago, Mamma, when you were talking about Evolution." What can a helpless American do with such bright children!

Mary suddenly understands that, as the Englishman's "distant cousins," the Americans were the same ancestry, according to another lesson, that started Evolution in the first place. Belloc makes no effort to clarify this implicit ambiguity of whether the American "cousins" were identical with those other "cousins," namely, the apes, who were, in 1925, held to be the origin of human life. Will Cuppy once wrote a book with the title, *How to Tell Your Friends from the Apes,* a title that flourished on the same amusing ancestral ambiguity.

Mrs. Markham "sharply" corrects Mary. The mother explains that she meant not what Mary implied but that the English themselves had descended from folks of Anglia and Saxonia. The English were really Germans! But Tommy next wants to know why did the Americans "branch off from us?"

Mrs. Markham is up to this question: "In the 17th century, my dear; that is three hundred years ago, for you must know that at this time the Government was so wicked that they would not allow people to worship God according as they felt inclined, on which account a number of noble men and women got into a boat called 'The Mayflower' and sailed away for a distant land where they might pray in the fullness of their hearts." But at this exalted explanation, Tommy only wants to know who "paid for the boat?" Mrs. Markham replies that they paid for it themselves. At which Mary observes that they must have been "very rich. Could you and Papa pay for a boat to take you over to America?" Mrs. Markham "hurriedly" changes the subject.

This wonderful history lesson about the origins of the Americans continues through the Pilgrims, slavery, the civil war, immigration, democracy, and the presidency. Mary inquires about the name of "the Governor of the whole United States." Mamma replies, "He is called President, my dear. Sometimes he is called one thing and sometimes another. The one who is president today is called Calvin." To which Mary replies, with obvious theological overtones, "Then, I am sure he must be a good man." "You are right, my dear," Mrs. Markham reaffirms the virtue of Mr. Coolidge.

Since it is during the late twenties, the subject of prohibition enters Mrs. Markham's discourse to her eager children. After explaining all the wonderful virtues of the Americans, Mary replies, "Really, Mamma, these people seem to have all the good qualities that anyone can possess." Mamma thinks it is time to explain to the children just how far American virtue extends.

> But I have not yet exhausted the list (of American virtues); for you must know that they have forbidden drinking wine or beer or any kind of thing on which anybody could get drunk, so that now no one in American knows even what Drunkenness is. And not only that, but they are now going to outlaw war, so that there will never more be war anywhere in the world, and no more shooting at people or dropping bombs on them from the air, or making them unhappy in any way.

How devastatingly amusing Belloc can be! On hearing of the arrival of this perfect world via the Americans, little Mary "(*dissolving into tears*) [says] 'Oh, Mamma, surely this is too good to be true'!!" And she "sobs" again.

From this exalted League of Nations mentality, things descends rapidly. Tommy wants to know why other nations do not copy "the noble example of the United States?" His mother explains, "It is in the mysterious designs of Providence; but you know, Tommy, that the world gets better and better, and therefore we may expect it to be as perfect as America is to-day."

After this remarkable explanation, Belloc notes "a Pause." Mary next wants her mother to name "the principal American Poets, Sculptors, Architects, and Theologians." Mary got the question from a book about Czecho-Slovakia. Mamma mentions a sculptor named Hiram Power. The poet is Longfellow. The principal theologian is "a lady called Mrs. Eddy." Do we detect a lacuna in perfection here?

Tommy's final question is noble: "Does everyone love America?" His mother has to tell the little lad that in truth only the English really love America. Other people "pretend" to love them, "notably the degraded French." The sign of this English love is that after all the money that the Americans doled out in the Great War, only the English are paying them back. This ingratitude of other nations infuriates Mary. "Then I hope, dear Mamma, the Americans will make war on all those wicked people and make them pay heavy interest as well!" Tommy adds sympathetically, "Yep! Blow >em out of the World!"

But Mamma reproves this bellicose sentiment against the lovely Americans who have made the world so perfect and who are their "cousins." "Nay! My dear children, these are not sentiments the Americans themselves would approve." They only use "peaceful forms of pressure such as those suggested by Mr. Otto Kahm." The obscure reference to Otto Kahm (Kahn), of course, is the final irony. He was an international financier whose "methods" Mrs. Markham probably thought to be worse than Mary's "make war on wicked people" or Tommy's "Blow 'em out of the World."

Such is the story of the "Americans," the "cousins" of the English, distant cousins of the Angles and the Saxons, if not further up the evolutionary ladder. Yes, as Mrs. Markham said, "the world gets better and better every day." Someday all can hope to be as "perfect" as the Americans are "to-day," i.e., in 1928, when drink and war were both happily prohibited. Now, we prohibit smoking. We pursue wars. Yet, some still demand "perfect peace." Oftentimes, I think Belloc's bemused parodies are not a little prophetic.

Chapter 20

"ULTIMATE KNOWLEDGE
UPON THE ULTIMATE REALITIES"

In 1927, Macmillan published a book by the Dominican philosopher, Vincent McNabb, entitled *The Catholic Church and Philosophy*. McNabb was a friend of Hilaire Belloc, whom he asked to write a brief "Preface" to the book. Belloc's "Preface" contains many points that are now found in John Paul II's *Fides et Ratio*, a document designed to address the condition both of philosophy in the present culture and of the importance of philosophy to Catholicism.

Belloc began his short essay by remarking that the one branch of knowledge that one would think "specifically pointed" to an area of interest to Catholicism, namely, philosophy, was most often seen as in "conflict" with it or "neglected" by it. However, at least one of the "peculiar functions" of the Catholic Church was to "preserve the philosophic conquests of pagan antiquity and to expand them over an even greater range of discovery than the greatest of the ancients had commanded." This is a remarkable sentence.

If the philosophic "conquests" of the ancients were to be preserved, it must imply that at least some of them were true, were worth preserving. But the other side of this preservation was to "discover" new understandings of reality using these same principles. This implied, however, that there was something in Catholicism that could add to, expand the understanding of these valid principles.

Religious conflict, Belloc thought, caused this relationship of philosophy to Catholicism to be obscured. Yet, everyone would grant that, say, in art or architecture, the religious experience of these traditions did add to their perfection. How account for this opinion that Catholicism did not also add to philosophy?

The problem has to do with the idea of "discovery," Belloc thought. In the modern world, the term "philosophy" has acquired a meaning quite different from its usage by the ancients or Christians. "Philosophy," Belloc succinctly comments, "signifies primarily the love of knowledge—*ultimate knowledge upon the ultimate realities*; and, by extension, it especially signifies *the solving of questions which the mind puts to itself relative to the most important subjects with which the mind can deal.*"

Man is a question-asking animal. Most people would have no problem with this affirmation. But it is peculiar to modernity, largely because of epistemological problems, to deny that any question, especially questions about the "ultimate realities," can have any coherent answers. What is clear for someone reading St. Thomas, for example, is that not only does he ask thousands of questions, he proposes thousands of answers, with reasons for his answers. With revelation, we are not as content, or at least not content in the same way, with Socrates' "knowing that we do not know." But there was no doubt that the ancients did ask penetrating questions about the highest things.

The term "discovery" means the processes or argument by which we find an answer to a question as asked. "A process of reasoning which establishes the existence of a personal God is a *discovery*." Belloc thinks that discovering a new philosophic truth is as important as discovering the planet Pluto or a physical law.

At first sight, many ultimate questions seem to be insolvable. This mood of frustration over the multiple contradictory answers given in philosophy gave rise to sophistry, as the Greeks called it. Sophistry meant giving answers just to be giving answers. It meant spinning out answers that seemed consistent or logical but which were really wrong or ungrounded. Sophistry, Belloc explains, "is the art of making up systems which do not really solve problems and which are hardly intended to do so by their authors, which are, in a word, not discoveries, but merely guesses at the best, or at the worst a mass of verbiage." A "mass of verbiage" would be a system with no basis in reality.

The sophist is the man who does not care about the truth or falsity of his position. He claims to be able to teach any system, whatever the questioner demands, usually for a fee. That is, he himself, the sophist, is not bound by any objective order of reality that would correspond or claim to correspond to his words. Indeed, he does not think there is such a thing as truth. This methodic doubt leaves him free to spin out any configuration he chooses, in secret or in public. The most dangerous sophists are those who seek to impose what is in effect their imaginations onto reality as if it were real. The sophist can teach the politician, hence the danger multiplied.

Belloc thought that this "sort of stuff," as he called it, has flourished since the end of the eighteenth century, especially in Germany. It is what most people today call "philosophy," a "theory" not a reality. The sophist, for instance, is someone who maintains that "there are no ultimate contradictions; any two apparently contradictory things may be resolved into a higher unity." Belloc calls such a position a "fog"! It sounds very much like Hegel, a German, to be sure.

The "glory of the Catholic Church," Belloc concludes, is "to have insisted throughout her existence upon the treatment of the gravest questions in a philosophical manner." And also, since the twelfth century, to have developed a "scheme of exploration" whereby some criterion of asking and answering such questions is in place. Since all of this questioning and answering has been going on for centuries, this genuine philosophic discovery must be seen for what it is.

At the time of the neo-Thomist period in which he wrote, Belloc could see some increasing interest in true philosophy. We are not looking for "the incomprehensible, the vague, nor the evading of questions in a mist of words, but research, discovery, and consequent rational and exact explanation."

What is to be noted in this brief philosophical preface of Belloc is his awareness of "discovery" and its criterion. He understood that valid questions were asked by the ancient philosophers, by Plato, Aristotle, and the Stoics. When these very questions were taken up in the light of revelation, they did not become less urgent or less necessary. Indeed, unless the questions were asked, unless the answers the ancient thinkers gave to them were known, no one would realize that the answers of revelation were in fact addressed to proper questions that had already arisen.

Modern philosophy is called sophistry to the extent that it systematically denies that our minds can reach reality and reason on this same reality, on *what is*. The charge of sophistry is accurate to the extent that modern philosophical systems do not base themselves on being but upon what the mind concocts for itself without any effort to ground its pronouncements in the valid questions and answers that have been proposed though experiment, reason, and argument.

Philosophy does concern itself with "ultimate knowledge upon the ultimate realities." The Catholic Church is indeed concerned with the philosophy that knows and seeks *what is*. It has insisted "upon the treatment of the gravest questions in a philosophical manner." When this treatment is not present, the education or the consideration is simply not Catholic, because it is not philosophical.

Part 5

"Different men have different pastimes, and I dare say that most of these who read this will wonder that such a search should be a pastime for any man, but I confess it is a pastime for me. To discover these things, to recreate them, to dig out on foot the base upon which two thousand years of history repose, is the most fascinating kind of travel."

—Hilaire Belloc, "The Roman Road in Picardy," *Selected Essays*, Methuen, 1948.

Chapter 21
BELLOC ON THE
METAPHYSICS OF WALKING

"There, the great Alps, seen thus, link one in some way to one's immortality. Nor is it possible to convey, or even to suggest, those few fifty miles, and those few thousand feet; there is something more. Let me put it thus: that from the height of Weissenstein I saw, as it were, my religion. I mean, humility, the fear of death, the terror of height and of distance, the glory of God, the infinite potentiality of reception whence springs that divine thirst of the soul; my aspiration also toward completion, and my confidence in the dual destiny. For I know that we laughers have a gross cousinship with the most high, and it is this contrast and perpetual quarrel which feeds a spring of merriment in the soul of a sane man."

—Hilaire Belloc, *The Path to Rome*, 1901.[1]

"The Greek word *philosophia* is a path along which we are travelling. Yet we have only a vague knowledge of this path. . . ."

—Martin Heidegger, *What Is Philosophy?* 1956.[2]

"There is not upon earth so good a thing as an inn, but even among good things there must be hierarchy. The angels, they say, go by steps, and I am very ready to believe it. It is true about inns. It is not for a wandering man to put them in their order, but in my youth the best inn of the inns of the world was an inn forgotten in the trees of Bramber."

—Hilaire Belloc, *The Four Men: A Farrago*, The Sailor, 1902.[3]

I.

If we be Platonists or Aristotelians, as I hope we are, we must, in some sense, also be peripatetics, that is, those who learn by walking about, usually about our cities if we be Greeks, about our countryside if we be English. Socrates is said to have left Athens only once, aside from the army, and that was a walk in the countryside described for us in the *Phaedrus*. Socrates asks Phaedrus where he has been and where he is going. Phaedrus replies, "I was with Lysias, the son of Cephalus, Socrates, and I am going for a walk outside the city walls because I was with him for a long time, sitting there the whole morning. You see, I'm keeping in mind the advice of our mutual friend Acumenus, who says it's more refreshing to walk along country roads than city streets" (227a). Socrates had no trouble agreeing with this preference for walking in the countryside on a hot day.

We should recall that Cephalus, the father of Lysias, was the elderly gentleman in the beginning of *The Republic* who was upset that Socrates did not come down to the Piraeus (seaport of Athens) to see him as Cephalus himself was old and could not easily get about the city any more. Socrates, however, protests that he enjoys talking to old men, for they can tell him how it is down along a path of life which we all must follow (328c-e). This passage reminds us that the very symbol of walking is itself an analogy for the path of our lives from conception to death and beyond—however vague our knowledge of its whole dimensions may be, as Heidegger reminded us. We have come from somewhere and we have someplace to go—as Chesterton said at the end of *Dickens*, the road ultimately leads to the inn, not the inn to the road.

Or, as Socrates puts it, "we might ask those who have travelled a road that we too will probably have to follow, what kind of road it is, whether rough or difficult or smooth and easy." Though Cephalus was rich, he still worried about his life, how he had lived it, what he must do to repair its errors. He obviously understood that the road led to a place to which he wanted to go.

I was born and raised in small-town Iowa, where walking in the countryside was part of my youth. I have lived much of my later life in three cities—Rome, San Francisco, and Washington—each of which is simply a walking city, a city of seeing and hearing. Each city must be seen on foot to see it at all—even of Los Angeles, the city of automobiles, I can only say that, in spite of its vastness, it is full of places in which it is pleasant to walk. Such cities do not allow us simply to "see" them. To see such cities, we must wander about them again and again over a long period of years. How did each city come to be? Why are we there, seeing it?—these are our questions. Walking is not mere exercise, though it is said to be good for us. We can, with a little effort, walk during most of our fleeting days.

II.

I do not visit a place, a city, a countryside, in which I do not try to walk, even if only for a time. I was once in Stamford, Connecticut, where I had forty-five minutes to walk its downtown streets. The noises, the spaces, the smells, the movements of people, of animals, of machines, all are important. Nothing assures us that a place is real more than walking in it, on its roads or its sidewalks or even its grass. When we put our foot down, the ground on which to step is already there. We did not put it there, nor less do we give ourselves the two feet with which we walk. Once we recognize that something is in fact "real," that it *is*, we can begin that second adventure of our existence, not only knowing that something besides ourselves exists, but of inquiring about what it means. *Omne ens est verum*. Without knowing, existence is not complete. For this latter project, as a sure guide, no one is better than Belloc.

"The love of a village, of a manor, is one thing," Belloc wrote in an essay entitled "On Old Towns." "You may stand in some place where you were born or brought up, especially if it be some place in which you passed those years in which the soul is formed to the body, between, say, seven years of age and seventeen, and you may look at the landscape of it from its height, but you will not be able to determine

how much in your strong affection is of man and how much of God."⁴
How much of our affection is of man and how much of God?—this too
is an ultimate question.

Just before her seventy-seventh birthday, my step-sister, Mary Jo,
then in Clarksville, Tennessee, told me that she and her son, one summer, hoped to stop in the town in Iowa in which we had gone to school
just so that her son, now a grown man, grown in other climes, could see
the houses and places in which his mother had once lived. This wondering about the physical dimensions of our origins is close to Belloc's
point. Even in ourselves, we cannot easily distinguish among those
things that are most important to us, which ones come from man and
which ones from God. In the project of knowing ourselves, it is not sufficient to know that we are born of our parents, though we do know this
immediate origin and want to know it.

This consideration, likewise, puts me in mind of the *Crito* of Plato,
of the famous conversation of the Laws of Athens with Socrates. The
personified laws remind him that the bond of marriage of his parents
was according to Athenian custom. Our very origins have something
about them that is already out of our control, the first meeting, accidental or divine, of our parents. This is particularly so if we hold, as, with
Plato, I do, that each soul that informs our particular body is immortal.
It is, moreover, directly created by the divine power alone. It does not
cause itself. Though we look like our parents, or our grandparents, the
light in our eyes is from eternity.

Thus, in encountering even ourselves, we encounter more than
ourselves. We cannot help but suspect that this grounding is beyond
our own powers. We know that our response to the Delphic command,
"Know Thyself," also directed at each of us, is at best inadequate. We
find out rather soon that in knowing ourselves, we must know first
what is not ourselves. We are not the direct object of our own knowledge. We know ourselves indirectly in knowing something other than
ourselves. We are set free to know by almost anything that is not ourselves. In this sense, all physical things transcend themselves in our
knowing.

But a walk in England, or France, or Africa, or Spain, or California,
each a memorable site of a Belloc walk, is not, at first sight, nearly as

solemn as our very births. Can we really speak of the "metaphysics" of walking? Metaphysics, after all, is a rather heavy word. We can so speak only, I think if walking puts us singularly in contact with reality, with *what is*, with what is not ourselves. Rousseau, in the Second of his *Reveries of the Solitary Walker*, writes:

> Having, then, formed the project of describing the habitual state of my soul in the strangest position in which a mortal could ever find himself, I saw no simpler and surer way to carry out the enterprise than to keep a faithful record of my solitary walks and of the reveries which fill them when I leave my head entirely free and let my ideas follow their bent without resistance or constraint. These hours of solitude and meditation are the only ones in the day during which I am fully myself and for myself. . . .[5]

Cicero had said, in III *De Officiis*, citing Scipio Africanus, that he was never less alone than when was alone.

But Belloc, who sometimes seems like a singularly lonely man, is closer to the truth. He is fully himself when the subject of his musings is not himself. Rousseau, on the other hand, almost seems to think that his freedom consists in removing real things from his reveries so that he can think without being grounded in or encumbered by an order of things not of his own making. Belloc's solitary walks are very different, I think, as we shall see.

III.

But a "metaphysics of walking?" Are we alone when we are alone? Cicero also said that he was never less idle than when he was by himself. Belloc, himself once a student at Newman's Oratory School in Birmingham, began his essay on the city of "Arles" in France in a way that almost only could be done by a Christian reader of the Greek classics, something that combines metaphysics and history, the knowledge of things and the things themselves.

The use and the pleasure of travel are closely mingled because the use of it is fulfillment, and in fulfilling oneself a great pleasure is enjoyed. Every man bears within him not only his own direct experience, but all of the past of his blood: the things that his own race has done are part of himself, and in him is also what his race will do when he is dead. . . . History, therefore, once a man has begun to know it, becomes a necessary food for the mind. . . . But history if it is to become just and true and not to become a set of airy scenes, fantastically coloured by our later time, must be continually corrected and moderated by the seeing and handling of *things*.[6]

Metaphysics is the science of being *qua* being, of first things and their causes. We are astonished that something, including ourselves, stands outside of nothingness. Even to meditate on nothing, we must begin with something not ourselves. Belloc probably would not have called himself precisely a professional metaphysician, if there is such a thing.

Yet, I was pleased to come across by chance, on the Internet of all places, the Preface that Belloc wrote in 1927 to Vincent McNabb's book, *The Catholic Church and Philosophy*. Belloc used the word "discovery" in connection with philosophy. He understood that he must make clear how this word, "discovery," applied to philosophy—itself an adventure in discovery of *what is*. At first sight, of course, if we "discover" something, it is already there; otherwise we fabricate it from what is there. That is, we do not, like much modern thought, concoct the content of what we think about out of our own minds. Our minds are certainly active spiritual powers, but they are initially, while still being minds, empty of content. And somehow, unless something already exists, we do not "encounter" it.

"Philosophy signifies primarily the love of knowledge—ultimate knowledge upon the ultimate realities," Belloc wrote,

> and, by extension, it especially signifies *the solving of questions which the mind puts to itself relative to the most important subjects with which the mind can deal*. Thus this word "discovery" is especially applicable to the philosophic function—the action of the mind when it succeeds in philosophical research. For instance, one of the prime questions man asks himself is whether his personality be mortal or not. The answer given to such a question is the supposed solution of a problem, and if the answer is true it is a *discovery*. Or again, a process of reasoning which establishes the existence of a personal God is a *discovery*.

Plato speaks of an *Eros* that compels us to seek to know the answers to the highest things. Notice that Belloc's emphasis is not merely on philosophy as a "questioning," which would make it merely a kind of misguided Platonism, but on answering questions, which bears hints of Aquinas. The real discovery is not that we have questions, but that we have answers to such questions. Our minds cannot be satisfied with mere questioning.

IV.

Needless to say, when one deals with Belloc and walking, he cannot forget either the inns at which he rested—recall the Inn at Bramber—nor that this inveterate walker was also a sailor—*The Cruise of the Nona* is his book on sailing around the British Isles. In the passage on Arles, as we have seen, Belloc never loses sight of the metaphysical need to "see and handle" actual *things*. We are to be constantly reminded that *things are*, that we cannot find out about unless we look at them, feel them. Belloc also reminded us that we are attached to the past and future of this very race of men to which we belong. In Belloc, if I may say so, the land symbolizes the reality that we know and need to examine. The sea is our call to something beyond ourselves.

"I never sail the sea but I wonder what makes a people take to it and then leave it again. . ." Belloc wrote in an essay entitled, "On Sailing the Seas."

> To sail the sea is an occupation at once repulsive and attractive. It is repulsive because it is dangerous, horribly uncomfortable, cramped and unnatural; for man is a land animal. .. A man having sailed the sea and the habit having bitten into him, he will always return to it: why, he cannot tell you. It is what modern people call a "lure" or a "call." He has got it in him and it will not let him rest.[7]

Belloc understood that within us there is indeed a "call," a "lure," yes, a "restlessness" that draws us out of ourselves. In spite of his concreteness, there is something almost Platonic about Belloc. He does not minimize the difficulties of sailing ships. He knows man is "a land animal."

Later in the same essay, Belloc is speaking of his "own small harbours of the Channel," places full of men who go to sea. Then he talks of the Morbihan, the land and coast of South Brittany and the peninsula of Quiberon. These latter men "produced vast ships rigged with iron chains, and boasting leathern sails, yet having nowhere, you would think, whither they could trade." What were they about?

The Romans, under Julius Caesar, Belloc tells us, once defeated these men of Morbihan in the waters "north of St. Nazaire." "But what a fight they put up! I think they must have gone to sea for the mere love of it, these men of the Morbihan, as do their descendants to this day. For they are all poor men and get little from their occupation beyond dreams and death."[8] The practical Caesar put to death the defeated sailors of Morbihan lest there be further naval threat from this direction. But I ask you, "is there a finer sentence in the English language than that this one of Belloc?" "For they are all poor men and get little from their occupation beyond dreams and death."

V.

Treves (Trier) is the oldest city in Germany, dating back to the time of Constantine. It is one town that is German that Belloc rather likes, mainly because it bears in its very foundation something older and larger than Germany itself. "All that great transition from the pagan to the medieval Europe one feels more at Treves even than one does at Aix; and this, I suppose, is because the roots of Treves go deeper; but partly, also, because Treves is more of a border town."[9]

Gothic had penetrated to Treves within a century after it arrived in Paris. Belloc went into the Church of Our Lady in Treves. He found there "something even more astonishing than its early witness to the Western spirit of Treves."[10] To the "left of the choir," he found a small freestone statue of Our Lady "of the most heavenly sort." No one had much photographed this statue; no one seemed to know much about it. But it was far better than the vulgar things he had seen in Metz, Berlin, Posen, and Leipzig.

Then Belloc gives us another insight into the metaphysics of walking, into the necessity of actually seeing and touching things, of allowing things actually to crash into our world:

> Seeing such a noble statue there, I thought to myself of what advantage it would be if the people who write about Europe would

really travel. If only they would stop going from one large cosmo-
politan hotel to another, and giving us cuttings from newspapers as
the expressions of the popular soul! If only they would peer
around and walk and see things with their own eyes![11]

We are to "peer around," "to walk," and finally "to see things with our
own eyes." But we live in a time when our epistemology often does not
allow us to trust our own eyes. We see but we do not believe that what
we see has its own existence.

VI.

The person most responsible for our not seeing what is there to be seen
is, no doubt, Descartes. In Belloc's *Characters of the Reformation*, he
devotes one chapter to Descartes (1596–1650) and one to Pascal
(1623–1662), both of whom he considers to be representative of the
philosophy that has formed modernity.

In the midst of these political figures, Kings and Statesmen and
Soldiers, whom we have been considering in connection with the
great religious struggle of the seventeenth century, we must run for
a moment to two men who had no political power. They were neither Soldiers nor Statesmen nor men of any hereditary position;
but they influenced the mind of Europe so greatly that their indi-
rect effect weighs more than the direct effect of others.[12]

Belloc saw the origins of "rationalism" in Descartes and of "emotionalism" in Pascal. Belloc notes that both men remained orthodox all
their lives, a sobering thought about the relation of faith and knowledge.

Belloc considered Descartes a great mind. From him we have "the
tendency in all philosophy called 'modern' which till lately grew more
and more skeptical of mystery, less and less concerned with the unseen,
and more and more occupied with matters susceptible of repeated experiment and physical appreciation."[13] Rationalism means that we only
know what is the product of our understanding of a method to know
what we examine. Thus, what we know is not really the thing examined
but what our method allows us to know and know in its terms.

As Belloc put it, "We mean by the Cartesian rationalism that habit of subjecting all examination of reality (that is, all search after truth) to a certain process which is called 'that of the reason' and 'the reason only.'"[14] Both Descartes and Pascal were "great mathematicians," that is to say, men who studied extended matter without motion. In both, especially things of the spirit became detached from examination of being.

In Descartes's method, he systematically eliminated from knowledge everything he could doubt until he finally arrived at what apparently he could not doubt, that is, his own existence. But even that certainty was based on the postulate that what he knew besides himself required, not a knowledge of real things, but a proof for the existence of a God who would not deceive us as the devil might. Belloc thought Descartes's postulate "I think, therefore I am" is true but it is the "postulate of a sceptic, and has acted ever since as a poison."[15] The "poison" prevents us from knowing the real relation of ourselves to what is not ourselves.

We are not only aware of our own existence. This is not the only thing that we cannot doubt. Belloc, in a profound passage, puts it this way:

> For there is another thing of which we are also just as certain, really, as we are of our own existence—and that is the existence of things outside ourselves. There is no rational process by which the reality of the external universe can be discovered; all we know is that it can be confidently affirmed. Aristotle, who might be called reason itself; St. Thomas, whose whole process was that of beginning with a doubt, and examining all that there was to be said for that doubt before the denial of it and the corresponding certitude could be arrived at, both postulate this second truth. Not only am I, I, but that which is not myself is just as real as I am, and what ismore, can be and is apprehended by myself.[16]

The "whole stream of modern skepticism" flows from Descartes. Belloc perceptively notes that one of the problems with modern European philosophy occurs when scientific evidence itself begins to suspect that the separation of "matter and spirit" is not as absolute as Descartes thought it to be.

114

VII.

This brings Belloc to Pascal. "Pascal began like a man moved suddenly by a vision or a great love."[17] Pascal made his reputation in dispute with the Jesuits of his time who "had made it their business to re-conquer Europe for the Church." There is an individualism in Pascal. There is a truth here. "In a sense the individual is everything; it is the individual soul that is damned or saved and the Church is only there to help a man to save it." But in emphasizing this majesty one can be led to belittle the divinity.

The Jesuits were thought by Pascal (and later by Nietzsche) to be too lax. Most people, Belloc thought, could make the proper distinctions between the law and the exceptions to the law. He knew the difference between murder and self-defense. Though he did anticipate that the emotionalism which he sees in Pascal had an ironic future. "It is worth noting, by the way, that the most sentimental people, who are loudest against the right to wage a just war, or execute a criminal, are just the people who are most likely to be in favour of 'putting incurables out of their pain,' which the commandment against murder most emphatically forbids."[18]

Belloc thought that Pascal's understanding the simultaneous greatness and misery of man was his greatest contribution. But he saw in Pascal's emotionalism the roots of a morality that ended up denying any objective order. "In Emotionalism the action of the conscience is not that of a deductive rational process, or even that of an experiment or of an appreciation of an object from without. It is an internal imperative order, which does not base itself upon a thought-out process or a deliberately sought experience, but on the immediate sense; it is an emotion, and nothing but an emotion, of right and wrong."[19] Belloc comments on the irony that both men remain in the faith, whereas their systems lead either to skepticism in the case of Descartes or, in the case of Pascal, "to a contempt for doctrine and a sort of cloud over the mind in which men lose the Faith."[20]

VIII.

Belloc's boat, to conclude his metaphysics of walking in the lure of a particular place, sailed into the port of Lynn, on the River Ouse, in

Norfolk, off the Wash into the North Sea. "Every man that lands in Lynn feels all through him the antiquity and the call of the town," Belloc observed.[21] Once ashore, Belloc was struck by the specifics of the place, its resistance to centralization.

There is something very English, or at least ancient English, about Belloc. "It is not only that the separate things in such towns are delightful, nor only that one comes upon them suddenly, but also that these separate things are so many. They have characters as men have. There is nothing of the repetition which must accompany the love of order and the presence of strong laws."[22] Men are each men and yet never the same. That there are so many particular things is itself a cause of wonder.

> Belloc had been in Lynn some nine years before his present visit. He wondered if the Burgundy wine at the Globe tavern was as good as he recalled it. Lynn was once called "Bishop's Lynn," but Henry VIII took it over to rename it, "King's Lynn." Belloc, however, still sees Gothic going back to the Bishop's times in the borough. "There is everywhere a feast for whatever in the mind is curious, searching, and reverent, and over the town, as over all the failing ports of our silting eastern seaboard, hangs the air of a great past time, the influence of the Baltic and the Lowlands." Even in failing, silting towns, we can find feasts for the eye if our mind is curious, searching.

"For these ancient places do not change, they permit themselves to stand apart and to repose and—by paying that price—almost alone of all things in England, they preserve some historic continuity, and satisfy the memories of one's blood." But there is a romanticism in Belloc that seems to suggest that wherever he might be, he will be refreshed by the being of what he finds. "So having come round to the Ouse again, and to the edge of the fens at Lynn, I went off at random whither next it pleased me to go."[23] All things are created good, and we should strive to know them as good.

X.

"For I know that we laughers have a gross cousinship with the most high."

"There is not upon this earth so good a thing as an inn."

"The great word *philosophia* is a path along which we are travelling."

"But you will not be able to determine how much of an affection is yours and how much is of God."

"History must be constantly corrected and moderated by the seeing and handling of things."

"Philosophy signifies the solving of questions which the mind puts to itself relative to the most important subjects with which the mind can deal."

"For they are all poor men and get little from their occupation beyond dreams and death."

"If only they would peer around and walk and see things with their own eyes."

"Not only am I, I, but that which is not myself is just as real as I am."

"I went off at random, whither it pleased me to go."

Chapter 22

ON THE LONELIEST MONTH

Somewhere, in Belloc's *Hills and the Sea*, which Scott Walter had once given to me, I recall reading a remark Belloc made about November, that it was "the loneliest month." I cannot now find this particular line or its context, look though I may. I was sure I had underlined it, as is my habit. At the time I read it, in any case, it struck me somehow with great poignancy, as Belloc often does. Perhaps because of Thanksgiving, and of the friends with whom I usually celebrate it, I have never quite felt that way about November, when the days do dwindle down, as the song goes. Even though he had an American wife, Belloc probably would not have much known Thanksgiving. Although its origins in a sense are from our English Pilgrim Fathers, Englishmen like Belloc would not have contrasted our Thanksgiving hominess with his loneliest month.

As I see it, a certain coziness hovers about November. We of the Northern Hemisphere are near to Winter. Days are short; evenings begin early, the shortest day still is in December. We live at a fortunate place on this revolving planet where seasons distinctly change and days noticeably lengthen or shorten. I remember being in Nairobi once for about a week. I was utterly dismayed by the idea that the sun would rise and set at almost the exact same hour of day every morning and evening of the year, exactly twelve hours. I recall once too being in Newcastle-on-Tyne at the Summer Solstice and marveling that the sun seemed to set for only a couple of hours. Months of such equal or long days, I suppose, do cause us to describe them as lonely or happy or unending or sad. Loneliness has the sense of missing human, and perhaps even more divine, company when it is wanted.

In 1776, Boswell recalls a period of the year in which he did not record, as was his usual wont, the exact time and place of many of Samuel Johnson's discussions. However, Boswell did have some notes about sundry diverse conversations that he grouped together as best he could (II, 35). On one occasion during this time, Johnson talked about the now contemporary and politically correct subject "of the misery which we cause to the brute creation." Johnson, however, knew of the argument that brute creation is compensated for any misery by existence itself. He recalled, to this effect, a remark of the Scottish philosopher—"the able and benignant Hutchinson"—who in his *Moral Philosophy* remarked that "if they (animals) were not useful to man, and therefore protected by him, they would not be nearly so numerous."

In spite of all we hear these days to the contrary, this observation of the Scottish philosopher is still closer to the truth than the opposite "vanishing species" fads we listen to from all sorts of nature funds. In fact, I heard Julian Simon talk the other day at the Cato Institute in which he pointed out that very few species are vanishing at all and that the vanishing of any species that do vanish has little to do with man. Man today, in fact, is involved in the counter-natural principle of preventing species from vanishing. Man is a curiously "unnatural" species.

Johnson, however, was judicious in thinking about this topic, or "topick," as he would write it. The question is, to be more precise, he thought, whether the animals themselves would, given such an alternative, endure existence on this condition of their misery caused by humans? We have to presume, on this supposition, that animals are not animals, but quasi-human beings with intellects and wills. This reflection led Johnson to recall, in this context, a comment of Madame de Sévigné. "Though she had many enjoyments, (she) felt with delicate sensibility the prevalence of misery." Madame de Sévigné thus complained "of the task of existence having been imposed upon her without her consent."

This distinguished lady, a copy of whose *Lettres à sa fille et à ses amis*, published in Paris in 1813, someone once graciously gave me, seems to have wanted to exist before she did exist in order to ascertain whether it was worth her while to exist or not. Presumably, if she judged, on the basis not of God's but of her prior analysis, that her own existence was not worth the trouble, she would then have continued to be nothing. I judge, on the same principle, that she would not have chosen to be an animal instead. Just how this blip of something in the midst of sheer nothingness could ever come to be to decide whether to exist, I have never been able to calculate.

This passage caused me, furthermore, to remember the month I once spent some thirty years ago, trying to learn French at Caen in Normandy, the home of Calvados and great cheeses. While I was there, I spent a good deal of time with a young German student, his wife, and little daughter. He was definitely a brooding, philosophic German young man. I remember him to have voiced the same complaint that Johnson recalled to me from Madame de Sévigné, namely, that he had not been asked whether he wanted to exist or not.

Trying to explain that the whole point of our existence is that it is not ours to choose to exist or not, remains one of those self-evident issues whereby, if you do not immediately see it, you will probably never get it straight. In his *Autobiography*, to this very point, Chesterton recalled, with approval, his grandfather's remark that he would thank God for his existence even if he were condemned to Hell. That position, in fact, may be more radical even than that of Madame de Sévigné and my German friend.

Obviously, I am on side of Chesterton's grandfather in this delicate matter, even as I am aware of the remark of the Lord about its being better to have a millstone tied around one's neck and be cast in the sea than to betray the Son of Man. Clearly, all of these are extreme cases. Indeed, the idea that we should first ask for our approval for our own existence before we exist just can never happen. It is one of those contradictions that serve to make a point about the nature of existence and choice itself. Presumably, God wanted us in existence; that is why we are here. Our prayer should be closer to that of Christ at His agony, to pray that this chalice pass from us, that not our will, but the Father's be done.

This brings me back to Belloc. In *Hills and the Sea (1906)*, one of the essays is entitled, "The First Day's March." Belloc's French army tour left a lasting impression on him in almost everything he wrote. After a day's march, the battery took its usual halt. Some commanders, Belloc recalled, like his own, preferred to have the men clean up a bit before going into the town, but others liked nothing better than "when they could bring their battery into town covered with dust and the horses screaming and the men haggard, for this they thought to be evidence of workman-like spirit."

Then two trumpets sounded the call known among the French as "the eighty hunters" (*"quatre-vingt, quatre-vingt, quatre-vingt . . . chasseurs"*). This call announced the approach of the large guns. The town was Commercy. As the troops went through the town, the little boys carefully watched "with pride." Belloc added, however, that these very boys did not yet know "how hateful they would find the service when once they were in for its grind and hopelessness." By contrast, Belloc added, that he himself had no way of knowing "the great pleasure he would have" ten years hence looking back on this very scene. Then Belloc added the point I want to make with regard to Madame de Sévigné: "Nobody knows beforehand whether he will like a thing or not; and there is the end of it."

Thus, in our November loneliness, the seasons shorten. We realize that to decide whether we would have chosen our own existence is a vain query. It is much preferable, as it were, to allow our existence to be freely given to us, given to us as a gift. To have chosen our own existence, it would not have been enough just to know about our existence and about our miseries. We would also need to know whether, in spite of it all, we might like an existence even if it be bound up with misery and suffering, as are all human existences. Scripture tells us that God Himself chose this way for His Son.

There is no way to decide this alternative beforehand. Even the existence of those who chose to be in Hell is a worthy existences. They are not created to be second-class citizens in the Kingdom of God. They do not and cannot deny their own goodness as God made them. What they do choose, as has often been said, is an ultimate loneliness, an exclusion of all else but themselves. This decision leaves themselves within a world of their own making.

No one knows "beforehand whether he will like a thing or not." This uncertainty is especially the case in November, the loneliest month, not because it reminds us of Hell, of only ourselves, but because it reminds us of that other loneliness which suspects that existence is a

121

gift even in the misery that inevitably follows with it, though does not constitute it. Existence is not, in fact, "imposed" on us without our consent. Our consent is, as it were, subsequent to and dependent on our prior existence. We cannot ourselves choose from out of nothingness to be ourselves drawn by ourselves from out of nothingness. If we could in fact do this, our loneliness would be absolute since we would be our own gods, precisely the condition of those in Hell.

Only if our existence is a gift, however, can we accept it as not coming from ourselves. Then we can suspect that we might in fact like this thing we call our own existence and that destiny which, as it were, called it from nothingness in the first place. As long as it is not we who call ourselves from nothingness, we can have hope. What we cannot, in any case, do beforehand, namely, decide ahead of time whether we will exist or not, we, when we think about it on a lonely November day, can give thanks for our existence, even for our existence in misery.

We are completely right to suspect that, this only existence there is, is designed for something that we could not possibly imagine beforehand. Our own choice would be based on our own resources and imaginations which are, by comparison with why there is existence at all, most paltry and limited. Belloc, like ourselves, ten years hence, a hundred years hence, eternity hence, had no idea of "the great pleasure he had looking back" on our existence and the misery connected with it.

Chapter 23

"IN THE PRESENCE OF SO WONDERFUL A THING"

Belloc's walks disconcert me. Not merely is one envious of when and where he walked—in Spain, in North Africa, across the United States, from Toul to Rome, in Sussex—but also of the time he took, of his memories. "History enlarges everything one sees," he wrote in an essay called "On History in Travel" (*Selected Essays*), "and gives fullness to flat experience, so that one lives more than one's own life in contemplating it, and so that new landscapes are not only new for a moment, but subject to centuries of varieties in one's mind."[1] Outside a room in which I lived for twenty years, there was a plaque informing me that "This floor was used as an auditorium from 1833–1879; it was used as a study hall from 1833–1889." This room embodies more than one's own life.

One evening, in Southern Spain, he tells us in "The Relic," in the same collection, Belloc had walked through a very dry and barren area, suddenly to come upon a huge Church that looked rather Italian to him. Though there were already some electric lights in Spain, the streets were dark. People in the few houses around the Church were sitting on the steps talking, but they were quiet as he walked into the town, obviously a foreigner. When he finally stood before the evidently huge Church, he confessed, "in the presence of so wonderful a thing I forgot the object of my journey and the immediate care of the moment and I went through the great doors."

The doors were elegantly carved. Belloc reflected a bit on how different and how similar were artistic works in Spain and Flanders. "The two districts differ altogether save in the human character of those who inhabit them. . . ." Flanders has meadows and woods, water. Spain was dry, a desert land, "with air like a knife, and a complete absence of the creative sense in nature about one." However, man's creative sense in both places "runs riot." All artistic details are completed in each place and are different from their neighbors. The "exuberance of the human soul" is revealed in both.

Within the Church is a central covered choir that takes one back to the earlier history of Christian worship. There, one has more the sense of the Byzantine, of the "Mysteries" that are separated out and highlighted in the choir. "In every Spanish church," Belloc explains, "you have, side by side with the Christian riot of art, this original hierarchic and secret thing, almost shocking to a Northerner, the choir, the Coro, with high solemn walls shutting out the people from the priests and from the Mysteries as they had been shut out when the whole system was organized for defence against an inimical society around." One thinks of our present Masses where almost nothing is shut out, where the Mystery at times almost seems to take a second place to fraternity, which should be its result, not its cause.

The stillness in the Church is not complete. Belloc sees a young priest at the end of the choir. Candles were lighted; people were murmuring, "though not at prayers." As he spoke no Spanish, he asked the priest in Latin, very slowly, whether there would be Benediction? But he did not know the Latin word for Benediction; so he called it "*Benedictio*" or "*Salus*." The priest nodded, "*Si, si*." However, what happens next is not Benediction. Rather, a middle-aged man comes out of the congregation to accompany the priest up the stairs. The priest takes a key and opens the door of an ornate cabinet. "The candles shone at once the rough thick clear glass upon a frame of jewels which flashed wonderfully, and in their midst was the head of a dead man, cut off from the body, leaning somewhat sideways, and changed in a terrible manner from the expression of living men." The head seemed very old.

Belloc realized that this devotion, the prayer before a relic, not Benediction, was common. "Our race from its very beginning, nay, all races of men, have preserved the fleshly memorials of those to whom sanctity attached. . . ." So Belloc is seeing something and in seeing it, he sees all of the races of men. He is miles from nowhere, does not speak the language, and is "in the inhospitable darkness of this hard

Iberian land." Yet, he does not feel like a pilgrim. He was more aware of awe, even terror, than anything else. He did not know the history of the face he saw, whether he was cut down by Mohammedans or by Pagans in the Pacific Seas.

The people said a few prayers in Latin, then the Our Father in the local tongue. "They next intoned the *Salve Regina*. But what an intonation!" Belloc knew this chant all his life, but the tune was new. "It was harsh, it was full of battle, and the supplication in it throbbed with present and physical agony." The graceful verses that closed the chant were "full of wailing, and the children's voices were very high." Belloc's reaction is unexpected: "Had I cared less for the human beings about me, so much suffering, so much national tradition of suffering would have revolted, as it did indeed appall me."

Finally, the priest closed the doors, locked them. A boy blew out the candles, "one by one," as Belloc recalled. He then went out into the market place in front of the Church, "fuller than ever of Spain." Notice the reason Belloc gives for not being "revolted" as seeing this distorted relic, this head from some unknown incident of sanctity. He does not deny that the scene is horrid.

But Belloc does realize that he is in someone else's land doing a thing common to all mankind, honoring the incidents of sanctity even if he did not know the particular story before him. But he "cared for the human beings about him"; he was in their Church, their land. He too knew the *Salve Regina*, but not in that melody. What is it he said? "In the presence of so wonderful a thing I forgot the object of my journey. . . ." This is the great capacity, isn't it? The capacity to stand before a wonderful thing, even in the desert of Spain, quite unbeknownst, and to recognize that even here are memorials of sanctity, of practices that all men share in their common lot.

Chapter 24
"WHAT WE HAVE LONG CALLED ENGLAND"

A nation has two existences, one in its on-going history, the other in its literature. Nations "rise and fall," we are told by a famous English historian, himself speaking not of England, but of Rome. In 1939, Herbert Jenkins Ltd. published a volume entitled *Week-End-Wodehouse*. This volume was reproduced "twice" in 1993 by the Pimlico Press on Vauxhall Bridge Road, in London. The Introduction to this book was written by Hilaire Belloc.

Evidently, Belloc had just been in that distant and obscure land called the United States where he was asked to do a radio interview on the "Trade of Writing." Belloc was quite astonished that this broadcast was heard by "some millions" of listeners. In this address, Belloc said that, bar none, at the time he was writing P. G. Wodehouse was "the best writer in England."

Naturally, such a selection created a good deal of "puzzlement" about why Wodehouse was "the head of my profession." Belloc took the occasion of this Introduction to explain why.

The first reason was that "writing is a craft." The examples of crafts Belloc chose to illustrate the point were "playing the violin, skating, batting at cricket, billiards, wood-carving," or "anything you like." The master of a craft is one who does what the craft does, only better than others, perfectly, in fact. Writing is a craft, the end of which IS to place in a reader's mind "a certain image and a certain emotion." This image and these emotions are put there by "the use of words in any particular language." Exactly the right words need to be used in the "right order."

The object of Wodehouse's craft is "comedy." He is out to make us laugh, and of course he does. He is a master at it. The reader is not supposed to see just how this end is perceived. If words are too odd, or images too convoluted, it is simply bad prose. Wodehouse was direct and simple in using words. He was extremely exact. Wodehouse was a master at analogies or what Belloc calls "parallelism." Thus when a formidable aunt came up to Bertie Wooster, he is pictured as "quaking like a jelly in a high wind." As this is to this, so that is to that.

A good writer is attentive to the "situation" of his characters. Wodehouse was a playwright as well as a writer of novels. "The situation, the climax, general and particular, the interplay of character and circumstance are all as exact as such arrangements can be." One is always satisfied when he ends a Wodehouse story. Everything has conspired to the end, to our delight.

Wodehouse wrote all of his novels with a stable set of characters. Many people have criticized this method, but Belloc thought it a virtue. Wodehouse set his plots in English country houses and clubs, and some in New York. In Wodehouse's novels, the vagaries of the young were "more human than those of their mothers." Wodehouse on the "club of the young," the Drones, could not be more amusing. Wodehouse wastes no adjectives.

Belloc is sure that Wodehouse has, in a way, seen all of the things he describes. The very heart of "all prose" is when what it describes rises up "almost violently before the eye to which it is presented." Belloc adds, "Those great masers of prose who the foolish think dull possess that power." Yet, we the foolish remember what we read.

To give an example of how a writer's vivid prose can cause an unforgettable impression in our memory, Belloc does not cite Wodehouse, but Newman, whom, I believe, he once met in Birmingham. The example he uses, perhaps surprisingly, is Newman's chapter on "The Arians of the Fourth Century." Even Schall recalls what Newman said about the Arians of the Fourth Century. This treatise on the orthodoxy of bishops was one of the principal reasons whereby Newman finally became a Catholic. Of course, Belloc would remember that passage while talking about Jeeves.

Some, Belloc thinks, may consider that stressing a man's style, rather than its content, even in English letters, is finally an "arid praise." Yet, Belloc ends with a final praise of Wodehouse, not unlike that of Chesterton's praise of Dickens. For Wodehouse had achieved the remarkable feat of creating "one more figure in the long gallery of living figures which makes up the glory of English fiction." In their literature, the English have created more living men and women in their literature than others. Wodehouse's unforgettable creation is Jeeves, the butler.

Of course, Wodehouse created other memorable figures, like Bertie Wooster himself, but Jeeves has that something "which may respectfully be compared to the work of the Almighty in Michelangelo's paintings. He has formed a man filled with the breath of life." No doubt, Belloc rather sadly foresaw, that "the race of butlers will die even sooner than other modern species." Jeeves, in our memories, is the leader of all the "gentlemen's gentlemen of the world."

Belloc's advice is to foreigners, as well as to posterity, who are, as he notes, but foreigners of another kind. They should "steep themselves in the living image of Jeeves and thus comprehend what the English character in action may achieve." But if the figure of Jeeves is doomed because the institution of the butler itself is gone, "will Mr. Wodehouse's work endure?"

We catch some of the mood of Belloc's soul here. He reminds us that "literary work does not necessarily endure through its excellence." Belloc was intently aware of the passingness of finite things. "What is called 'immortality' (whereas nothing mortal is immortal!) is conferred on a man's writings by external circumstances as much as by internal worth." Many nations are filled with those who never knew Keats, while many of those who read French find Racine to be merely "dull."

Wodehouse was famous when Belloc wrote. He still is. But whether his fame will remain depends "alas, upon what happens to England." As England chooses to make itself more and more "multicultural" and "open," does its new population read Wodehouse?

Belloc even left us a prophecy on this score in 1939. "If in, say, 50 years Jeeves and any other of that great company—but in particular Jeeves—shall have faded, then what we have so long called England will no longer be."

It is now some seventy years since Belloc wrote these lines. I read on Google that publishers in 2008 plan to republish forty-two titles of

P. G. Wodehouse. This is almost only reassurance I have these days that England is safe.

I recall someone once wrote that, in his old age, Belloc himself read nothing but the *Diary of a Nobody*, P. G. Wodehouse, and his own works. I suspect that England would be even safer if he added the other two items to its reading list, not neglecting Jeeves and his friends.

Part 6

"I took a slower train, which came immediately behind it, and stopped at most of the stations. I took my ticket rather at random for a little station between Pont de l'Arche and Mantes. I got out at that little station, and it was still early— only midway through the morning. I was in an odd mixture of fatigue and exhilaration: I had not slept and I would willingly have done so, but the freshness of the new day was upon me, and I have always had a very keen curiosity to see new sights and to know what lies behind the hills."

—Hilaire Belloc, "Home," *Selected Essays*, Methuen, 1941.

Chapter 25

THE CHARM OF BELLOC:
"ON CARING TOO MUCH"

"But I noticed only this morning, turning over one of her pages, a charming and comforting reflection. She says of one of the men in her books that one of the women in her books who came across him paid no attention to what a certain gentleman thought of any matter because she did not care enough about him—not in the sense of affection but in the sense of attention. So speaks this ambassadress from her own sex to mine, and I will not be so ungenerous as to leave her without a corresponding reply.

"My dear Jane Austen, we also do not care a dump what any woman thinks about our actions or our thoughts or our manners unless they have inspired us to—what shall I call it? It need not be affection, but at any rate attraction, or, at least, attention. Once that link is established, we care enormously: indeed, I am afraid, too much."

— Hilaire Belloc, "Jane Austen," 1941.89

I.

The title of this Chapter is "The Charm of Belloc." The title is redolent of Plato. Plato's *Republic* was written to counteract the charm of Homer on the Greeks. Plato knew that no mere philosopher could ever command the attention that a poet could command. His recourse was to combine poetry and philosophy into one single book, the *Republic* itself, whose charm we all know, or if we do not, we do not belong to the civilization that I address here. Plato sought to "out-charm" Homer.

Do I think Belloc was another Plato? What I do think is that he had to do substantially the same thing. For the false ideas about the gods a true idea had to be found and made loveable. Few would read "proofs for the existence of God" and understand them. But they might order their souls correctly if they sang, if they heartily sang the music of the real gods. Belloc sang a lot. His writing is charming. Beware of him, for his charm has sparks of the same allure of Plato, though in the service perhaps of a different God, or better, of one who, by the time of Belloc, had let us know who He was. Thus, Belloc could sing in the *Four Men*: "And thank the Lord / For the temporal sword, / And howling heretics too; / And whatever good things / Our Christendom brings, / But especially barley brew!"[2] Revelation is about thanking the Lord, about the things of Caesar, about the heretics who deny Trinity and Incarnation, and those who tell us that the good things of this earth are evil, even when they are good. We thank God for beer and wine, as Chesterton, I believe said, by not drinking too much of them. Aristotle said this also, such is the sanity of both.

To introduce anyone, to anyone who has the happy fortune to read such a book as this *The Quotable Hilaire Belloc*, is to introduce him to the whole world, to what happened in it, and to what lies beyond it. But in so reading this book, we memorably pass through the world itself, through its towns, rivers, inns, and cities, through the homes of men, to where they fought each other, where they loved, where they argued late into the night about *what is*.

Often the passage is on foot, or in a boat, or sometimes it consists in just sitting quietly at the "George," the Inn at Robertsbridge, "drinking that port of theirs and staring at the fire." Here, in the mind's eye, there arises "a vision of the woods of home and of another place—the lake where the (river) Arun rises."[3] Belloc was a wanderer who loved to be at home, two virtues kept together only with the greatest of delicacy, but both belong to our being in this world.

The purpose of Hilaire Belloc, I mean that of his existence in this world, is to be sure that what is solid, the "permanent things," do not pass us by, even when they are not of our time or of our place, embedded as they usually are in the most ephemeral of things, among which things we ourselves stand outside of nothingness. Belloc teaches us that, unless we set down in print, yea in print, the places we know, the people we love, the things that amuse us, they will disappear, even in our efforts to remember them. "As a man will paint with a peculiar passion a face which he is only permitted to see for a little time, so will one passionately set down one's own horizon and one's fields, before they are forgotten and have become a different place. Therefore it is that I have put down in writing what happened to me now so many years ago. . . ."[4]

We are given our own lives to live and we must live them in our time and place. We have friends, but, as Aristotle said, we cannot be friends with everyone as the risk of having no friends at all. But one life is not enough. We must live other lives. We can best do this "more living," I think, by following Belloc in what he called "the towns of destiny," in the history of England and France, along the path to Rome, yea, even into the "servile state" and the "characters of the Reformation."

Belloc was a man of England, a man of France, a man of Europe, yes, a man of the world. He was, I think, the best short essayist in the English language. How often have I thought of Belloc's sailing out of the port of Lynn. "So having come round to the Ouse again, and to the edge of the Fens at Lynn, I went off at random whither next it pleased me to go." Where it pleased Belloc to go "at random" is always a place worth seeing, a place we could not now see without him.

And what had Belloc seen in Lynn? "For these ancient places do not change, they permit themselves to stand apart and to repose—by paying that price—almost alone of all things in England they preserve some historic continuity, and satisfy the memories in one's blood."[5] What a remarkable expression that is, to "satisfy the memories of one's blood." Our memories, to be ours, must be more than those memories we have only of ourselves. Our blood remembers our grandparents, our ancestors, the kind of being we are whose soul and body mysteriously belong both to eternity and to our forefathers who begot us.

Belloc was a sad man. He lost his American wife, whom he loved dearly, in 1914, a son in each of the great wars of Europe. Yet he was a man who laughed much and enjoyed the companionship of men and the mystery of women, about whom, as he said in his lovely essay on Jane Austen, we care "enormously," even at times "too much." On the day before he reached the town called Borgo, he reflected on such things in the *Path to Rome*":

> All you that feel youth slipping past you and that are desolate at the approach of age, be merry; it is not what it looks like from in front and from outside. There is a glory in all completion, and all good endings are but shining transitions. There will come a sharp moment of revelation when you shall bless the effect of time. . . . All you that have loved passionately and have torn your hearts asunder in disillusions, do not imagine that things broken cannot be mended by the good angels.[6]

Do not imagine that things broken cannot be mended. This is the essence of redemption, of the civilization built on the Nativity.

Still the life we are given, we must live. Belloc tells us, on October 30, 1902, on his walk in Sussex, that "The worst thing in the world is the passing of human affection. No man who has lost a friend need fear death . . . It has been said that no man can see God and live. Here is another saying for you, very near the same: No man can be alone and live. None, not even in old age."[7] And Belloc lived into old age. Born in 1870, he died in 1953. It is said of him that in old age, in his home at King's End as a lonely old man, he read but three books: Boswell, the *Diary of a Nobody*, and his own works. One cannot help but be amused at this list, or doubt that most of what is worth knowing is contained in them.

The diary of Mr. Charles Pooter, the famous "nobody" who resided at "The Laurels, Brickfield Terrace, Holloway," begins with this dedication: "Why should I not publish my diary? I have often seen reminiscences of people I have never even heard of, and I fail to see—because I do not happen to be a 'Somebody'—why my diary should not be interesting." In spite of his someone hundred and fifty books, Belloc may have seen himself at a "nobody." Needless to say, his diary, his accounts of what he sees and thinks are indeed "interesting," to use a mild word for them.

The diary ends with Pooter dreaming that one of his friends kept taking a crown off his head. He handed the crown to Pooter and addressed him as "President." He seems to have been in the "White House of Washington" where he must wear his crown. Belloc and Chesterton thought the American presidency was indeed the "last of the medieval monarchies."[8] At this, "We all laughed long and very loudly, till I got parched, and then I woke up. I fell asleep, only to dream the same thing over and over again."[9] Belloc perhaps learned from Mr. Pooter, the famous "nobody," that often the same things need to be dreamed over and over again. Reading Belloc often allows us to do precisely this reading over and over again.

II.

To read Belloc, one must, I think, be capable of being what I call "delighted" about the very fact of existence. It strikes me that the best way to read this *The Quotable Hilaire Belloc* is first to catch something of his charm, his nostalgia, his sadness, yes, his delight in things. Belloc wrote a letter from King's Land to Maurice Baring on February 6, 1911.[10] Baring himself was a distinguished English diplomat, a long-time friend of both Belloc and Chesterton. His collection *Lost Lectures* is one of the most amusing books I have ever read.[11] A famous painting of Belloc, Chesterton, and Baring can be found in the Tate Gallery.

I am not sure just from whence Baring was writing to Belloc. In his response, Belloc disagreed with something Baring said. In Baring's letter, Belloc found "a touch of Devil-worship about it," a serious concern indeed. Devil-worship evidently means ultimately denying that existence itself is good, not unlike classical Manicheanism, though it only denied that matter is good, not being itself.

To make his point, Belloc presented to Baring a sort of litany of "do's" and "don'ts" to explain just how the Church itself acted in dealing with reality. The Church says simply as a command, "Don't kill." The Church does not say, "If you kill, regard it as a sacrament." However, in saying "Do not kill," there are exceptions. One exception is just war. There the Church blesses the banners of the Armies. Preventing killing is not murder.

The Church does not say, "Do not marry." Belloc observes that the

Church has difficulty in dealing with normal human relations "in a prohibitive way." What the Church does say about the marriage is that it is "indissoluble." The Christian praise of the celibate life has nothing to do with whether "marriage is right or wrong," just as, Belloc adds in a striking comparison, preferring a professional to a conscript army tells us nothing about whether a given war is just or unjust.

Belloc sees the Church's teaching on celibacy in this manner: If you are going to deal with the "inner life," you had best be celibate. The Church adds that if you are going to deal with the "inner lives of others and direct and administer them, you must really be celibate." Belloc adds that this last practice is not a dogma, but it is discipline. The relation between the celibate and married life is not a question of degree of holiness, but of "two different kinds of life, both approved." Because of its very nature of dealing with one's own and others' inner lives, one is more "spiritual than the other."

Nor does the Church say, "Do not be rich." She does warn that wealth is dangerous and can easily corrupt. This is merely a statement of observed fact. But as such, being rich tells us nothing of someone's "character." We cannot conclude from the fact that riches are dangerous to whether a given rich man is actually corrupt. He may in fact be quite virtuous. When no Church is present to counteract the normal false assumptions about riches, Belloc observes, "People always think that great wealth indicates something: Intelligence at the lowest and courtesy or some other virtue at the highest." But of itself great wealth indicates neither intelligence nor courtesy. Belloc adds that the Church soberly warns us about wealth: "Unless you use it with the greatest care and worry yourself to death about it, you are doing a direct injury to your fellow citizens." Belloc calls this simply "sound economics."

Then Belloc adds, in an example that probably does not follow, "Every time you (Baring) and I drink champagne, we are ultimately depriving some poor man of beer, and don't you forget it." This quip of Belloc, however, is not "sound economics." It is best forgotten. In a market economy, we are more likely to deprive a poor man of his beer if we do not drink champagne. But of course, Belloc adds with some playfulness, that in fact at that moment, at least, he does not enjoy champagne. So on his own terms, there is no danger in his drinking it and upsetting the flow of beer to the poor man, which beer, be it noted, Belloc thinks, the poor man has a perfect right to drink if he wants.

Belloc's stomach is upset. He does not think that he likes any "wine" except "Herefordshire Cyder." Just why he calls "cider" "wine," I am not sure, for surely Belloc of all people, with both French and English blood in his veins, knew the difference. He did not, consolingly, seem to worry about whether the champagne that he and Baring might drink would deprive the poor man of "Herefordshire Cyder."

"What is all of this leading up to?" you might ask. So far we see little of the devil here. But he is hanging around fuzzy ideas, as his wont. Belloc continues, "As for the Church saying 'Don't exist,' that is the last of the series and is absolutely plumb flat contradictory." The Church cannot approve of something that is "absolutely plumb flat contradictory." Faith does not contradict reason, as Aquinas often put it.

If you want to get Belloc's point, try to command something before it exists, not to exist. We do not have the power of existence as such in our arsenal. This is the great Thomist truth, the truth of existence. Existence is the Gift we do not give ourselves, but only receive it. This is why, from our side, to recall Belloc's friend Chesterton, gratitude is the first response to being.

Belloc sums up these teachings: "The Church does say definitely, 'Don't kill.' She certainly thinks sex dangerous, she regards riches with the utmost suspicion. But existence she delights in and it is Catholic civilisation only that ever produces a strong sense of individual existence." This is the most marvelous of sentences. *To delight in existence itself*, this is the highest mark of sanity and reality. If we can delight in existence itself, we can, even more, delight in the tiny particular being that exists—the "strong sense of individual existence."

Belloc gave us in 1911 a criterion against which to test his thesis: "Let a nation lose the Church, and it is bound to fall in time into Pantheism, or a denial of spiritual continuity, and the immortality of the soul." We no longer bury our dead. We kill our kind before they are born and hasten their ends when they are useless. We deny that past generations can bind us to anything, no Constitution, no natural law. We subsume all back into Earth. We judge individual existence merely as a function of or threat to the Environment, not as the peak of worldly existence itself. We can no longer, it seems, smoke indoors or out of doors. We have reinvented prohibition and made killing the tiniest of our kind a "right."

Thus, with regard to economics, I do not see why the rich and the poor both cannot have champagne, beer, or Herefordshire Cyder. And with regard to the Devil-worship that Belloc worried about in Baring's letter, what Belloc caught was a rancid smell of the idea that existence itself is not good, and hence that life is not good, that sex is not good, that material things are not good. In the affirmation that the Church "delights in existence," he knew that, however gingerly we must some-times treat them, because of what they are, all things, as it says in Genesis are good. And we are to delight in them in their proper order, in their being.

III.

The reading of Belloc, as I say, charms. "Look you, good people all, in your little passage through the daylight," we are advised in "The Death of the Wandering Peter." "Get to see as many hills and buildings and rivers, fields, books, men, horses, ships, and precious stones as you can possibly manage to do." This seeing of all that we can find is one way to live our lives. But it is not the only way, nor is it necessarily the most exciting one.

There is an alternative: "Or else stay in one village, and marry in it and die there. For one of these two fates is the best fate for every man. Either to be what I have been, a wanderer with all the bitterness of it, or to stay at home and hear in one's garden the voice of God."[12] We again recall Belloc's love of home, his love of wandering. We can, we suppose, find the voice of God in either choice of path, but we must lis-ten, even in our own garden

In his book on the great French Revolutionary figure, Danton, Belloc recounts the scene of Danton's execution in Paris on April 5, 1794. It is another place for the voice of God to be hears. Danton, the notorious Director of the Committee on Public Safety has fallen from power. The Revolution is eating its own. It is a moving, sober account that Belloc makes alive for us:

Danton was the last. He had stood unmoved at the foot of the steps as his friends died. "Trying to embrace Hérault before he went up, roughly rebuking the executioner who tore them asunder, waiting his turn without passion," Belloc wrote,

> he (Danton) heard the repeated fall of the knife in the silence of the crowd. His great figure, more majestic than in the days of his triumph, came against the sunset. The man who watched it from the Tuileries gate grew half afraid, and tells us that he understood for a moment what kind of things Danton himself had seen. By an accident he had to wait some seconds longer than the rest; the executioner heard him muttering, 'I shall never see her again . . . no weakness," but his only movement was to gaze over the crowd. They say a face met his, and that a sacramental hand was raised in absolution.[13]

In a footnote, Belloc tells us that Louise Gely was the second wife of Danton. They were married by the Abbé de Kéravenan le Breton, whose hand is said to have finally absolved the great anti-Christian revolutionary. As I say, he who reads Belloc reads ultimate things.

The last pages of *The Path to Rome* ends beautifully. Like Socrates in his final oration to the jury in Athens, Belloc spoke to those who would read his book after his time. This is now, for a while, our time. "And now all you people whatsoever that are presently reading, may have read or shall in the future read, this my many-sided by now ending book; all you also that in the mysterious designs of Providence may not be fated to read it for some very long time to come . . . ." to all of these, Belloc says "Farewell."

But before he does, Belloc again reminds us of the truth of earthly things in which we now spend our passing years. "Human companionship once broken can never be restored, and you and I shall not meet or understand each other again. It is so of all the poor links whereby we try to bridge the impassable gulf between soul and soul." I know of no passage that, by humanly despairing the attainment of the highest of human things, hints of what eternal life must be.

Belloc, of course, ends *The Path to Rome* by singing doggerel. "Across the valleys and the high-land, / With all the world on either hand, / Drinking when I had a mind to, / Singing when I felt inclined to; / Not ever turned my face to home / Till I had slaked my heart at Rome."[14] This passage is mindful to me. It talks of home and Rome. When I finally left Rome after my twelve years of teaching there, I wrote an essay "On Leaving Rome."[15] I remember saying in that essay that Rome was a place that was familiar to us even if we had never been there. It is in our "blood memory," it is in our companionship, our sacraments, our wine, our very faith.

The existence of Belloc means that we each have a path, a journey, and it leads to Rome if we would but take it. The charm of Belloc is not that he did not despair of himself keeping on this path. It is that of some things, like ladies who attend to us, he cared too much, and in such manly caring he reached the source of the Love that alone causes us to care at all. In this spirit, Danton's absolution too had something to do with the face he saw from the steps of the block.

Belloc was a modern man who was a man of faith, both. The two are not contradictory. He knew his philosophy. "I found my cigar and lit it again, and musing much more deeply than before, not without tears, I considered the nature of Belief. Of its nature it breeds a reaction and an indifference. Those who believe nothing but only think and judge cannot understand this. Of its nature it struggles with us. And we, we, when our youth is full on us, invariably reject it and set out in the sunlight content with natural things." But once tried, the natural things do not satisfy us. "All these beautiful things," as Augustine said, point beyond themselves. And Belloc loved the beautiful things he found in his walks, in his sailings, and in his home.

And do we, once having strayed, return? We can and some do. "What is it, do you think, that causes the return? I think it is the problem of living; for every day, every experience of evil, demands a solution. That solution is provided by the memory of the great scheme which at last we remember."[16]

"No, Belloc, in the end, we cannot care too much," we exclaim, "now that we have read you. You lead us to the important things that few in our time will speak to us about." We too are lonely.

But you still speak to us in those towns of destiny, in the man who saw "what Danton saw," in the Port of Lynn, in the county of Sussex that you call home. We still listen, those of us who read you. We remember "the great scheme" of which you spoke there in the Alps. You had just been in the village where they knew the "psalms very well," but their Latin sounded "more German than French."

The men and women sang the salutation to God that begins: "*Te, lucis ante terminum, (Rerum Creator, poscimus . . . .).*" "To Thee, before the close of day, Creator of the world, we pray. . . ." Even if we do not hear "*Te, lucis ante terminum*" in our churches, as Belloc heard it sung in the mountains in 1901, we still sing this hymn, we, the men and the women for whom men care perhaps too much, sing it to ourselves, those of us who read you.

Again, such is the charm of Belloc. You who, in these pages, read him "in the mysterious designs of Providence" are fated to find out, even if it is "a long time to come" before you find him on his paths in this world.

Chapter 26

OCTOBER THIRTIETH, 1902

October 30, 1902 was the second day of Belloc's walk through Sussex in *The Four Men*. Sussex was "the first place to be created when the world was made." On this day, of which I like to read every year, after spending the night at the Inn at Robertsbridge, Grizzlebeard and Myself meet the Sailor and the Poet—each of whom is Belloc himself. Myself explains to the Sailor that he is walking westwards to "to Arun and to the land I know."

This delightful chapter contains the story of how St. Dunstan cheated the Devil by making the local roosters awake a half-hour early, a trick much to the Devil's annoyance. It might be dangerous to cross the Devil, but St. Dunstan knew "the Devil's way." He "always pretend(s) that he is the master, though he very well knows in his black heart that he is nothing of the kind."

Here too is found the account of the Squire of Brightling who went to Parliament, a man by the name of Fuller. Fuller was called to "order" by the Speaker for speaking too long, but he refused to yield the floor. At that restriction on his freedom, Fuller marched right out of Commons back to Brightling, a hero, where he subsequently spent "all his great fortune upon the poor of Sussex and of his own parish, bidding them drink deep and eat hearty as being habits the best preservative of life, until at last he also died." There was "honour" in being the Squire of Brightling, but "no honour whatsoever to be a member of the Commons House."

The recurrent question of the Thirtieth of October, however, was more profound than Parliament. It asked: "What was "the worst thing in the world?" The Poet suggests that the worst thing in the world is trying to light a fire with "a smoking chimney." The Sailor, who is trying to light the fire, replies that this is nonsense. "Death," he affirms, "is the worst thing in the world."

But Grizzlebeard rejects this position also. "The worst thing in the world is the passing of human affection. No man who has lost a friend need fear death." It is this theme that I want to follow in this account of the Thirtieth of October, 1902. I know of no more poignant topic.

The Sailor responds blithely that he has made and lost lots of friends, recalling one in Valparaiso, but he saw "no great tragedy in it." Grizzlebeard replies that this is young man's talk, not serious. What he is concerned with is rather the gradual "weakening" and "severance" of human bonds. He adds, "it has been said that no man can see God and live. Here is another saying for you, very near the same: 'No man can be alone and live. None, not even in old age.'"

One suspects a certain profound poignancy here in Belloc himself. We should recall that Belloc seems to have been the most companionable and gregarious of men. This theme of loneliness is not that of someone who has no friends. This makes the theme doubly mysterious.

Grizzlebeard talks about something of human experience. "Absolute dereliction is the death of the soul; and the end of living is a great love abandoned." The Poet thinks that, with time, all things heal in their place. Grizzlebeard agrees.

Yet, there is a problem. Grizzlebeard even uses the words "condemned to live" for those who have this experience of a great love abandoned. What can he be getting at? Evidently, death can be endured and life goes on. The abandoned loves create a different issue. What? This is especially perplexing if we recall that love is beyond justice. We cannot command it or its continuance—even though, to be itself, it has this anticipated permanence about it.

This is Grizzlebeard's explanation: "Everything else that there is in the action of the mind save loving is of its nature a growth: It goes through its phases of seed, of miraculous sprouting, of maturity, of somnolescence, and of decline." Evidently, everything but loving is subject to this natural process. Why is loving not included?

"But with loving it is not so; for the comprehension by one soul of another is something borrowed from whatever lies outside time: It is not under the condition of time. Then if it passes, it is past—never grows again; and we lose it as men lose a diamond or men lose their honour." To love, we must first be loved. It often strikes without preparation, without anticipation. Love, especially at its deepest levels, is a gift, an undeserved gift. It is not merely a response to *what is*, but affirms it. It is "outside time," as Grizzlebeard remarks. This timelessness of love and companionship must mean that we are caught up in loving with something beyond ourselves. We do not create it. It seems to create us.

The Poet is taken aback by the vehemence of Grizzlebeard's gloomy affirmation of love's passingness. He chides him. The toothache is the worst thing in the world. The Sailor corrects him, no, "it is the earache." But Grizzlebeard thinks both are "talking like children." He repeats his thesis: "The passing of human affection is the worst thing in the world." It is not the same as death. People do not die of their own choosing. The passing of affection has something to do with choosing, for human companionship is a mutual choosing, a reciprocity, as Aristotle already told us.

But Grizzlebeard, in spite of what he has said, does have a place for "decay": "But the decay of what is living in the heart, and that numbness supervening, and that last indifference—oh! these are not to be compared for unhappiness with any other ill on this unhappy earth." What does this sentence imply? The ultimate unhappiness is not death but rather something gone wrong in the bonds of companionship, friendship, and love.

Myself wants to know if this loss of companionship is a thing of old age. Not necessarily, though the old know it too. However, "when the enthusiasms of youth have grown either stale or divergent, and when, in the infinite opportunities which time affords, there has been opportunity for difference between friend and friend, then does the evil appear." Love is not free of vicissitudes.

Belloc describes how such things come about, almost a deception of the effects of original sin. Men will disagree over who is guilty or not. "The one man loves a war, the other thinks it unjust and hates it (for all save the money dealers think of war in terms of justice). Or the one man hits the other in the face. These are violent things. But it is when youth has ripened, and when the slow processes of life begin that the

146

danger of the certitude of this dreadful thing appears: I mean the passing of affection. . . . Unless communion be closely maintained, affection decays."

Myself begins to talk of "irrevocable things." He brings up the opposite of the worst things. "For in the midst of this wood, where everything is happy, except man, and where the night should teach us quiet, we ought to learn or discover what is the best thing in the world." Of course this is the theological question that follows logically from the question of the worst thing in the world. "I am a little puzzled in this point: why, if most men follow their satisfaction, do most men come to so wretched an end?" They discuss whether digging a hole and filling it up again—the ultimate act of human purposelessness—is "the true end of man and his felicity." It is, no doubt, if there is no answer to the question of human companionship and its passingness.

Finally the Poet tells us, to return to our theme, that the best thing in the world "is a mixture wherein should be compounded and intimately mixed great wads of unexpected money, new landscapes, and the return of old loves." If the loss of human companionship is the worst thing in the world, surely "the return of old loves" is the best, however unexpected. If they are gifts in the first place, not products of natural growth, "how do they return?" we wonder.

In his Apostolic Letter, *"Mane Nobiscum Domine"* (October 7, 2004), John Paul II wrote, "this relationship of profound and mutual 'abiding' (Eucharist) *enables us to have a certain foretaste of heaven on earth. Is this not the greatest of human yearnings?"* The object, surely, is not simply the "foretaste," be it on earth or in heaven.

"What is the worst thing in the world?" "What is the best thing in the world?" What is the "greatest of human yearnings?" The answers given to these questions are, respectively, the loss of human companionship, the return of old loves, and the yearnings that are not merely "foretastes," however valid said foretastes are. But how do they occur and return? They are "outside of time" we are told. They do not grow like natural things. St. John said that God has first loved us. That we are loveable is not something that we give ourselves. Plato said that we can be struck by a beauty that we did not know existed and be beside ourselves, suddenly knowing that *something is*. It is of these things that we meditate on the Thirtieth of October, 1902, when we encounter Myself, Grizzlebeard, the Poet, and the Sailor

The last words are those of the Sailor: "For when I see the grave a long way off, then do I mean to put on slippers and to mix myself a great bowl of mulled wine with nutmegs, and to fill a pipe, and to sit me down in a great armchair before a fire of oak or beech, burning in a great hearth within sound of the Southern Sea."

Two days after October 30th is November 1st, All Hallow's Day. What All Hallow's Day celebrates, the Communion of Saints, is the only ultimate answer to "the worst thing in the world."

Chapter 27

IN PURSUIT OF NOBODY

This all started when I needed some sort of quotation suggesting that, lacking all else, civilization needed but two books, the Bible and Shakespeare. Searching my highly fallible memory, I vaguely recalled something that a young friend had written to me about a passage in A. N. Wilson's book on Hilaire Belloc. I had in fact read the Wilson book, and according to my memory, that was the perfect quotation! I recalled it as reading: "In his last days, Belloc read nothing but the Bible, Shakespeare, and his own works." Naturally nothing could have been more perfect for my purposes at the time.

I was next recounting this incident to another friend, who, it turned out, admired my memory but quietly hinted that there was something wrong with it. She was rather sure that this was not an accurate quotation except about Belloc's reading his own books.

So I finally resorted to the facts and located Wilson's book. The passage reads in Wilson as follows:

> Mr. Belloc himself . . . shuffles about between the study and the kitchen and the chapel, and his bedroom. His reading now consisted entirely of *The Diary of a Nobody*, his own works, and the novels of P. G. Wodehouse, which he would read with the satisfied intentness of an old priest poring over his breviary.

About this time, I thought that, well, perhaps civilization might just also be saved if instead of reading the Bible, Shakespeare, and Belloc's own works, it still read Wodehouse. But what was this *Diary of a Nobody*? How could that save civilization?

I had never heard of it. I went over to the reference desk of the Lauinger Library on our campus. I looked through the card catalogue, or perhaps the computer contraption that is now there to help you search for what should exist. I believe I finally found, in one of the early editions of the *Encyclopedia Britannica* under "Diary," a reference to this book and the name of the authors. They turned out to be two English brothers, George and Weedon Grossmith, who had originally published this book in *Punch*, in the 1890s.

George Grossmith evidently had something to do with Gilbert and Sullivan. Indeed, he turned out to be one of the original pillars of D'Oyly Carte Opera Company. George Grossmith was Jack Point in *Yeoman of the Guard* and the First Lord in *H. M. S. Pinafore*. Things were looking up. But our library did not have this book. I thought of trying inter-library loan, but by chance one of the reference librarians found that the book was still in print by Penguin.

So I hustled down to Olsson's Books and Records then on Wisconsin Avenue. This was sometime in the summer. They did not have the book either but ordered it for me. Weeks passed, months. I went down every so often to inquire if it had arrived yet, as I was really curious to see the book. Finally, a very nice salesman told me, looking sadly at his computer, that the book was not available.

Sometime later, however, Scott Walter told me that he was on some sort of English booklist and noticed that *The Diary of a Nobody* was available. He asked me if I wanted it. I did. So for Easter Sunday I received an extremely handsome edition of *The Diary of a Nobody*, published in London in 1969 by the Folio Society, with an Introduction signed merely "J. H." and drawings by John Lawrence. I believe Weedon Grossmith did the original drawings.

Belloc is said to have thought this book "one of the half-dozen immortal achievements of our time" (originally published in 1892). This "J. H." more quietly says of it that it is "a minor masterpiece of unmalicious humour."

In the "Book World" of the *Washington Post* for April 2, 1989, moreover, there was a section on "Recommended Reading" that contained a brief notice by James A. Causey on, of all books, *The Diary of a Nobody*. Mr. Causey wrote: "Whenever you feel your life is mundane, when you think you hear twittering behind your back at the office or when you are treated rudely by some store clerk half your age, bring your problem to Mr. Charles Pooter (hero of *The Diary*). He has never let me down yet." The "twittering" settled it.

Several years ago I wrote a pamphlet for the Catholic Truth Society of London entitled *Journey through Lent*. The section on Holy Week was called "The Unsuccessful Man." (Chapter 30 of this book.) I had forgotten about this until Scott reminded me of it and its source, which is, of course, from Belloc's poem "The Unsuccessful Man." This poem concludes: "Prince, may I venture (since it's only you) / To speak discreetly of the Crucifixion? / He was extremely unsuccessful too."

Now that I think of Belloc's love of this *Diary of a Nobody*, it seems that he saw in it a kind of Christ figure, of the fallible and failing man who somehow was the object of redemption. And it seems clear why Wodehouse would find himself in the same category. When Belloc read these books with the attention a priest should give to his breviary, perhaps he was engaged in a prayer for all those "nobodies" of whom the world is mostly composed, including himself, his own works.

When I recalled hearing of this passage in Wilson, when one friend told me of it, and another remembered it better than I, I was merely amused and delighted. But now I wonder if this amusement and delight did not portend that close connection of delight and sadness that Belloc understood so well, that is the very heart of the Incarnational world in which we live.

I will not recount the contents of *The Diary of a Nobody*. It is about the life of a man whose worldly affairs never quite go right, even though his is quite a good man and leads a normal life. The distance between his self-respect or dignity and how the world sees him is almost infinite. Life cures him of his illusions and therefore makes him the more poignant and in fact more decent.

On April 29, for example, Charles Pooter, a successful third-level businessman, has been having trouble with his son, Lupin. Lupin has at the time no decent job, is living at home and has other—to his father—odd ideas. Pooter's wife, Carrie, is quite lovely but, maternally, she often has to side with the son. A couple of friends, Gowing and Cummings, come over as is their wont. Pooter, to liven things up, decides to tell them about his extraordinary dream. He had a dream of blocks of ice on fire, and it "was so supernatural that I woke up in a cold perspiration." Pooter was quite moved by his dream.

To this major event in his father's life, Lupin answered, "What rot!" Gowing added that "there was nothing so uninteresting as other people's dreams." Pooter appeals to Cummings, but he too had to admit that Pooter's "dream in particular was especially nonsense!"

Pooter replied: "It seemed so real to me." To this, Gowing retorted: "Yes, to you, perhaps, but not to us." And the *Diary* adds: "Whereupon they all roared." The reader cannot help but feel sorry for poor old Pooter, even though his dream was indeed boring.

During all of this, Carrie, Mrs. Pooter, was quiet, only to add finally to her husband's dismay: "He tells me his stupid dreams every morning nearly." Exasperated, Charles responded: "Very well, dear, I promise you I will never tell you or anybody else another dream of mine the longest day I live." At this good news, Lupin yelled: "Hear! Hear! And helped himself to another glass of beer."

The subject was then dropped, and finally the Nobody's great dream and its recounting were forgotten when "Cummings read a most interesting article on the superiority of the bicycle to the horse." The Bible, Shakespeare, Wodehouse, Belloc's own works, and *The Diary of a Nobody*—these all are full of the Prince and the nobodies for whom The Unsuccessful Man lived and died.

Chapter 28

BELLOC'S INFAMOUS PHRASE

No phrase was more excoriated that that of Hilaire Belloc: "Europe is the faith and the faith is Europe" (1924). Yet, what John Paul II and Benedict XVI say about the origins and meaning of Europe, in contrast to the denials of the European Union, suggest that the faith did found Europe. The faith is the origin of Europe as a coherent unity of various non-civilized tribes seeking to live together in one Church and one Empire yet retaining their own customs and boundaries.

David Goldman, in his book, *It's Not the End of the World; It's Just the End of You,* put it this way: "Hilaire Belloc's famous quip—'Europe is the faith and the faith is Europe'—is precisely correct."

Europe is where Old Testament, New Testament, Greek, and Roman traditions melded with the so-called barbarians coming largely off of the Eurasian continent. This fusion did not happen overnight, but it did happen. Europe's unity was hammered out in thought from the Fathers of the Church to Aquinas. The Reformation was not so much an argument against this thesis, but about its origins. Luther's problem with Aristotle was a harbinger of divisions to come.

Up until recent times, most people, Europeans or otherwise, looking at the continent saw the obvious fact. Catholic origins united that not-so-large land mass under common assumptions about what life, liberty, God, man, and cosmos were about.

Some wanted to make a distinction in early modernity. The "scientific revolution" was something anti-Christian. Yet, the world-wide "conquest" of science was but an aspect of that generalizing and universalizing movement of intelligence that was already in Europe from its classic traditions.

Modern science itself has Christian medieval origins. Without the understanding of a real world, itself not God, worth investigating together with the notion of real secondary causes, no science would be possible. Those societies that embraced a voluntarist origin of things never developed science because one cannot investigate what can constantly be otherwise.

What was especially abjured about Belloc's statement was the second part—"the faith is Europe." This was taken to mean that Christian missionary endeavor was to transform other non-Christian societies into something looking like Europe. As later commentators point out, Belloc was factually correct. While pockets of Christians exist in many parts of the world, the Chinese, Hindu, and Muslim portions of the world remain largely as they were in terms of numbers of Christians.

Many, including Goldman, note the rise of a kind of house-based Christianity in China that may include as many as one or two hundred million people. Moreover, the Chinese along with Hindus, Koreans, Japanese, and other Asians have rapidly mastered science and technology. This fact might seem to prove the modernist thesis that science needs radically to be separated from religion. What it better proves is that reason is universal, just as Belloc indicated.

The heart of this question today can be found in Benedict XVI's "Regensburg Lecture." What was unique about the early Christians, the pope indicated, was that they did not first address their efforts to other religions. Rather they were first concerned with the philosophers. Paul went over into Macedonia; he did not turn East to India, as is the tradition about the Apostle Thomas.

If we add to this consideration that, already in some of the books of the Old Testament, we had attention to *Logos*, the famous "I am who am" of the Mosaic definition, we find that Christianity considers itself both to be in a real world, wherein human action makes a difference, but also to be, because of its origins, a faith that addresses itself to reason.

Christianity is sometimes considered to be a Greek "myth" about a suffering God. Rather it conceives itself to be the recipient of a revelation of the Trinitarian God who was incarnate as the Logos of His inner life into this world, true God and true man. This happened during the reign of Caesar Augustus.

No doubt, the inner dynamism of Christianity was to "go forth and teach all nations." It was assumed that reason was common to all men, however much they did or did not recognize it. The purpose of the mission was salvific, to explain the ultimate meaning of each person in the world.

But in the light of this explanation, the *Logos* was to discover and allow to develop the "reason" that was found in each culture. Many things could be retained, some things rejected, but that was not because they were imposed but because they were unreasonable. This was what Belloc's second element of his aphorism meant. Unless it chooses, no culture is in principle immune from reason. No culture is immune from the *Logos* addressed, to complete it, to that culture's own good.

Chapter 29

HARBOR IN THE NORTH

The last essay in *Hills and the Sea* is entitled "The Harbour in the North." The essay begins: "Upon that shore of Europe which looks out towards no further shore, I came once by accident upon a certain man."[1] As far as I can determine this unnamed harbor is on the northeast side of Scotland looking north to the Orkneys and the Arctic Ocean. Belloc had sailed into this little harbor and dropped anchor in low tide. In the silence of the morning, he heard a man "crooning" to himself. He spotted him in another boat nearby at the sea-wall. The boat was "sturdy and high, and I should think of straight draught. She was of great beam. She carried one sail and that was brown," Belloc carefully tells us.[2]

Belloc struck up a conversation with the man. The man answered, "in a low and happy voice." He said, "I am off to find what is beyond the sea." Belloc naturally wanted more particulars: "To what shore?" The man again replied "I am out upon this sea northward to where they say there is no further shore." The man seemed to have a plan. He had prepared for a long voyage.

The man had something almost mystical about him. Belloc asked him about the voyage. The man replied:

> "This is the Harbour in the North of which a Breton priest once told me that I should reach it, and when I had moored in it and laid my stores on board in order, I should set sail before morning and reach at last a complete repose." Then he went on with eagerness though still talking low: "The voyage which I was born to make in the end and to which my desire has driven me is towards a place in which everything we have known is forgotten, except

156

those things which, as we know them, reminded us of an original joy. . . ."[3]

The man also said that there was also a harbor in the South.

The man, however, does not know the happy people there, but thinks they shall receive him. He has specific directions about this harbor from which he now sails. When he reaches his destination, he says, "I shall come off the sea forever, and everyone will call me by my name." The sun was just rising but Belloc did not have a good look at the man, though he thought by his voice he was from "the West." The man was in fact from Cornwall, not Brittany or the Islands.

Realizing that what this man seeks is something transcendent, Belloc tells him, "You cannot make this harbour; it is not of this world." Just at that point, the wind rose and the man sailed out of the Harbor in the North. He may have been going to Norway or the Orkney Isles. He kept a steady tiller till he was out of Belloc's sight. Belloc then concludes both the essay and the book in the following exalted manner:

> "Oh, My companions, both you to whom I dedicate this book and you who have accompanied me over other hills and across other waters or before the guns in Burgundy, or you others who were with me when I seemed alone—that ulterior shore was the place we were seeking in every cruise and march and the place we thought at last to see. We, too, had in mind that Town of which this man spoke to me in the Scottish harbour before he sailed on northward to find what he could find." (220).

No doubt "that Town" of which the two spoke in that Harbor was the one of which Augustine spoke. The poets and the philosophers, at their best, also tell us of such things.

But, in the end, Belloc tells us, quite soberly, yet with that utter realism that knows the true location of the City of God: "But I did not follow him, for even if I had followed him I should not have found the Town." As Augustine said, the City of God, the "Town" of God, is not in this world. But that does not mean, contrary to Machiavelli, that it does not exist. Nor does Belloc imply that it doesn't exist, only that he, like the sailor in the harbor in the North, is not there yet.

Chapter 30

THE UNSUCCESSFUL MAN

Good Friday is surely an awesome day. Perhaps no other day of the liturgical year requires of us the same kind of silence, aloneness. We fast almost by instinctive forgetfulness because we are absorbed in listening to John's account of the death of Jesus. Sometimes, if we are lucky, we can listen quietly to Bach's Passion according to Matthew or that according to John. We share in the special emptiness of the church when it is stripped at the end of the Good Friday liturgy.

Somehow, in our confused logic, we always feel that this ought to have been otherwise, that it did not need to turn out in quite the way it did. And we are not wholly wrong in this. God could have found another way to redeem us. Hilaire Belloc wrote this famous epitaph for himself: When am dead, I hope it may be said: His sins were scarlet, but his books were read. More soberly, he also wrote a poem in 1923, "The Ballade of Unsuccessful Man":

Prince, may I venture (since it's only you)
To speak discreetly of the Crucifixion?
He was extremely unsuccessful too.

The Holy Week liturgy recalls that lovely ancient refrain: *"Christus factus est obediens, obediens usque ad mortem, mortem autem crucis."* Christ was obedient, obedient even up to death, to the very death of the Cross. And this obedience seemed to lead to a kind of failure.

It is not easy, in recounting Christ's trial before the Judgment Seat, which was so clearly unjust, to judge who is responsible, who not. Christianity, however, does not allow us, even now, to sit by and watch. For we were there, and our Good Friday liturgy enables us to behold ourselves there somehow, somewhere amidst the crowds and principal participants.

The Jesuit poet Gerard Manley Hopkins wrote these lines after a text from Jeremiah:

Thou art indeed just, Lord, if I contend
with Thee; but, sir, so what I plead is just.
Why do sinners always prosper? and why must
Disappointment all I endeavour end?

When we look clearly at the Calvary scene of Good Friday, of course, we cannot but be startled that disappointment should have been allowed to mar the enterprise of God. Unless we think it all some kind of play-acting—that Jesus really was not there or that he was some kind of ethereal spirit—we know all this ought not to have happened. Yet, what are we to conclude in our silent watching the fallibility of God, the intractability of men? How could Christ have been so unsuccessful? God must be a little less than omnipotent, perhaps?

Nonetheless, as we watch, we know the Christian tradition does not think him unsuccessful. When he cried out at the end that it was consummated, we know he did the will of his Father, that will which chose to redeem us only after the fashion of our freedom. We watch Pilate on his judgment seat being told that he would have no authority to execute anybody were it not given him by the Father. We recall the Supper of the evening before when Jesus told his disciples he was going to his Father. There seems to have been a plan here, a rationale.

We each are to be defined by what we think of this Crucifixion. There are many who have never heard of this drama, yet, we know that there are also men and states who work diligently to prevent it from being known. Principalities and Powers still seem to surround it, for it remains the crucial drama for mankind. Plato, the greatest of the Greek philosophers, said, almost prophetically, that if a truly good man ever appeared on this earth, he would be hounded, scourged, and finally impaled. We can, of course, get angry at such an outcome and insist on creating a society in which such an event could not happen. Were we only there, we tell ourselves, it would have been otherwise. Some insist this was the lesson Christ came on earth to teach.

Yet, I suspect, Good Friday is probably not meant to tell us how much better it might have been were we there with *our* plans, *our* political theologies, *our* righteousness—we, and not Pilate and Caiaphas

159

and Peter. Plato was closer to the truth and so was Augustine later on. The starkness of Good Friday, like all of Lent, is meant to lead us to the Father. We shall find no other way but Christ's.

The unsuccessful man, then, did succeed. But another "Day" is needed for this. On Good Friday in about A.D. 29, a few minor Roman and Jewish officials put to death one Jesus of Nazareth, a carpenter's son, so it was said, though others claimed he was a king. On that day, nothing could be seen except his lack of success.

CONCLUSION

In the beginning of this book, I cited six brief quotations from Belloc's various works—from 1) *The Cruise of the Nona,* 2) "The Hill of Carthage," 3) "On the History of Travel," 4) "The Approach to the Sceptic," 5) "The Channel," and 6) "The Death of Wandering Peter." Further, at the beginning of each part of the book, I cited more of Belloc: Part 1, "On Cheeses," Part 2, "Courtesy," Part 3, *The French Revolution,* Part 4, "Boswell," Part 5, "The Roman Road in Picardy," and Part 6, "Home." These passages remind me of the enormous range of Belloc's interests. They always also touch on his spirit, on the soul of a man very much alive in this world. He was a man who knows that he is made for this world but it is never enough. To think that it is sufficient to us undermines the very notion of what it is to be a human being.

And the reflections on his readings are how I "remember" Belloc. Everywhere or anywhere amidst the hundreds and hundreds of books, essays, and poems that he wrote, we find passages that stop us, awaken us, and make us think of things we never appreciated before or, if we have noted them, we are alerted to a new way of looking at what we already knew. We cannot avoid what time does to us, Belloc tells us on the cruise in his boat. Yet, knowing this, we can find peace in God's will for us. Mortals we are, who are also "immortals," as Belloc also says.

And as he looks at the ancient power of Carthage, redolent of Hannibal and the great wars with the Romans, Belloc tells us that things, nations and empires, as well as men are fragile. The great empires of the Carthaginians and the Romans are no more, though, on his walks, Belloc thinks that much of Rome is still alive. He tells us that we see much more if we know what happened in a place that may look uneventful to us now. Our mind must also see what our eyes observe in order that we might understand it.

We are not to be skeptics, Belloc tells us. We are to distinguish between the meanings of words. We realize that the same word can have different meanings, both of which we can understand. Belloc had little sympathy for the stupid insofar as they thought themselves to be wise. The man who tells us that God would not allow us to lose our souls does not understand the radical freedom that God has given to us. Such a man understands little of the reaches of free will or its temptations. God did not make men free only subsequently to prevent them from choosing to love or reject Him. The free decision to love or reject Him is, in fact, the drama of our existence in all times and places.

Belloc tells us of an experience, a "glamour of the mind," that transforms us when we see the origins of things. What are the "origins?" The "beginning" was spoken of in Genesis and in the Prologue to John. We cannot think of things that exist without wondering about their origins. And if things have origins, they also have ends. They are not static, even when we see them in the moment of time in which they are given to us to see them. How true it is that few of us know where to find the meaning of the beginning of things, the order of things, and the end of things.

We, "good people," pass through the "daylight." It takes but a short time. We are to see the "hills and buildings and rivers, fields, books, men, horses, ships and precious stones," as many and as long as we can. We often pass by these things every day without marking them. Yet, we do not all need to be world travelers, out to conquer the world by seeing it, stepping on every land and walking every path. The man or woman who stays at home, who marries, and dies in his village may well see best the most important of things in his own garden. The voice of God is there too. Belloc finds a "bitterness" in the wandering man, perhaps because he is slow to remember that all wandering begins and returns to home.

The return to home was, as we have seen, both what *The Path to Rome* and *The Four Men* were about. Chesterton had said in *Orthodoxy* that the primary experience that Christianity explained to him was "how we could be homesick at home?" If we have never been homesick, we cannot be human, really. And our homes are like our loves. Indeed, our loves are what make homes possible. We find that in their very reality, both our homes and our lives lead us beyond ourselves, as if we are most incomplete when we are most complete in our human dwellings and living.

In the essay on "Home" at the beginning of Part 6, Belloc tells us of his curiosity for new sights. He wants to know "what lies behind the hills." And in his essay "On Cheeses" that begins Part 1, we find that the variety of things is what most manifests the Spirit. Only six great cheeses have been produced outside Europe. But we find 253 different kinds between "the Ebro and the Grampians, between Brindisi and the Irish Channel." We suspect, moreover, that Belloc tasted every one of these 253 different kinds of cheese, so eager was he for being, for *what is*. The splendor of creation includes the existence of many different, wonderful things, each with its own distinctness.

We often hear our lives compared to a journey, we are "wayfarers and pilgrims" going home or seeking to establish one. But why cannot we see what is there along the way? Belloc tells us of the Roman Road in Picardy at the beginning of Part 5. The best time we have is usually our "pastime." We discover what is there. We re-create what was once there. We do this in our minds and books. We remember. What is the basis of what we see? The "most fascinating" kind of travel is that which covers time as well as space. We are not alone in this world, but we tend to forget those who have walked before us. They have given us a real world if we "dig out on foot the base upon which two thousand years of history repose."

When I consider the thinkers who have moved me most—Plato, Aristotle, Augustine, and Aquinas—I always add Chesterton and Samuel Johnson. So I am pleased that Belloc wrote an essay on Boswell, whose biography of Johnson is simply the best, the most memorable account we have of a human life in all its wonder. At the beginning of Part 4, Belloc tells us that no one else could have lived Johnson's life and no one but Boswell could have recorded it. When we realize this, Belloc tells us, we begin to see that our lives are not simply "chance" events. "Chance" is the wrong word for them. The right word is closer to "Providence," a providence that includes our free wills, our foibles, our sadnesses, our joys and blessings, and yes our judgment.

I have included but one of Belloc's poems, that he called "courtesy." It is at the beginning of Part 2. He tells us that it is less than courage and less than holiness. He touches here on the theme of Flannery O'Connor's *Mystery and Manners.*[108] Belloc tells us that it is on his "walks" that he realizes that "the Grace of God" is "courtesy." That is the great medieval word. It is the word that is beyond force and laws. It is the kindness that sees the destiny of each member of our kind and responds to it. This courtesy is why Belloc's essay on "Jane Austen," to which I often referred in these pages, is so moving.

And finally, at the beginning of Part 3, I cite a passage from Belloc's book on *The French Revolution*. It is a brief passage, mostly about political prudence. But its principle is about revelation and its need to be itself, to have institutions that allow it to be what it is. For in our ultimate remembering of Belloc, we include the supernatural religion that he saw even on his walks in the mountains, hills, rivers, and valleys of Europe.

Revelation tells us about ourselves when we have exhausted all other ways of learning about ourselves—who we are, what is our destiny. It is about what is always new in the world. At first, it sounds strange to say that what is old is ever new. But that is only because we do not understand the abidingness of the things *that are*, the things that have been handed down to us. We begin to understand them, however, when we think all we can with our own powers, only to find that we are knowing beings who do not know everything that we need to know to understand who and what we are.

Belloc's inns and towns, his songs and walks, his loves and sadnesses are remembered here. As I say, we often ourselves run into the ultimate things because we have read a writer who brought us to them. Belloc does this "bringing to" again and again. He is a man of this world who is a Christian. In the end, this added newness of revelation is the only way to be a man who really knows the world as it is, with its glories and disappointments, both.

"Remembering Belloc" is not an exercise in biography or history. Rather it is an exercise in seeing *the things that are*. Belloc told us what he saw not just so that we also see and remember things we would otherwise miss, but that we too might see what is about us, its glory and its doom. Belloc knew in what sense Christ was "unsuccessful too." The phrase that I remember best is "the immortality of mortal men." This twofold presence is indeed our status in being.

The final words are the ones I love from the Preface to *The Four Men*: "And as a man will paint with a peculiar passion a face which he is only permitted to see for a little time, so will one passionately set down one's own horizon and one's fields before they are forgotten and have become a different thing." In "remembering Belloc," we too recall the faces we are permitted to see only for a brief time and the fields we knew before they became different things. These too are the basis of our rejoicing that we are the mortals whose end transcends our very mortality.

SELECTED BIBLIOGRAPHY

Baring, Maurice. *Lost Lectures, or the Fruits of Experience*. New York: Knopf, 1932.

Belloc: A Biographical Anthology. Edited by Herbert van Thal and Jane Soames Nickerson. London: George Allen & Unwin, 1970.

Belloc, Hilaire. *Battleground: Syria and Palestine*. London: Lippencott, 1936.

_____, *Characters of the Reformation*. Garden City, N. Y.: Image, 1961.

_____, *Cranmer: Archbishop of Canterbury*. Philadelphia: Lippencott, 1931.

_____, *The Crusades*. Milwaukee: Bruce, 1937.

_____, *Cruise of the Nona*. Boston: Houghton-Mifflin, 1925.

_____, *Essays and Poems*. London: Dent, 1938.

_____. *Essays of a Catholic*. London: Sheed & Ward, MMXXXI.

_____, *Essays of To-Day and Yesterday*. London: Harrap, 1928.

_____, *Europe and the Faith*. London : Constable, 1924.

_____, *Four Men: A Farrago*. London: Nelson, n. d.

_____, *Four Men: A Farrago*. Introduced by A. N. Wilson. Oxford: Oxford University Press, 1984.

_____, *French Revolution*. London: Williams & Norgate, [1911] 1927.

_____, *Great Heresies*. New York: Sheed & Ward, MCMXXXVIII.

_____, *Hilaire Belloc's Stories, Essays, and Poems*. London: Dent, 1957.

_____, *Hills and the Sea*. Marlboro, Vt.: Marlboro Press, 1906.

_____, *Life of Danton: A Study*. London: Nelson, n. d.

166

_____, *Miniatures of French History*. Peru, Il. Sherwood Sugden, 1990.

_____. *On Nothing & Kindred Subjects*. London: Methuen, 1908.

_____, *The Path to Rome*. London: Nelson, n. d.

_____, *The Path to Rome*. Garden City, N. Y.: Image, 1956.

_____, *Places*. London: Cassell, 1941.

_____, *Richelieu*. Garden City, N. Y.: Garden City Publishing Company, 1929.

_____, *Selected Essays*. Edited by J. B. Morton. Harmondsworth: Penguin, 1958.

_____, *Selected Essays*. With an Introduction by J. B. Morton. London: Methuen, 1948.

_____. *Servile State*. With an Introduction by Christian Gaus. New York: Holt, 1946.

_____, *Silence of the Sea*. New York: Sheed & Ward, 1940.

_____, *Sonnets and Verse*. London: Duckworth, 1923.

_____, *Towns of Destiny*. Illustrated by Edmund Ware. New York: McBride, MCMXXVII.

_____, "Truth about Modern Art," *Collected Works of G. K. Chesterton*. San Francisco: Ignatius, 1989. XXXII.

_____, *Wolsey*. Philadelphia: Lippencott, MCMXXX.

Bloom, Allan. *The Closing of the American Mind*. New York: Simon and Schuster, 1987.

Camus, Albert. *Lyrical and Critical Essays*. New York: Knopf, 1968.

Chesterton, G. K. *Charles Dickens*. New York: Schocken, 1965.

Copper, Bob. *Across Sussex with Belloc: In the Footsteps of 'The Four Men.'* U.K: Sutton, 1995.

G. K.'s Weekly: A Sampler. Edited by Lyle W. Dorsett. Chicago: Loyola University Press, 1986.

GKC as MC. Edited by J. P. de Fonseka. Freeport, N. Y.: Books for Libraries Press, 1967.

Grossmith, George and Weedon. *The Diary of a Nobody*. London : Folio Society, 1969.

Heidegger, Martin, *What Is Philosophy?* Translated by J. Wilde and W. Kluback. New Haven: College & University Press, 1956.

Jaki, Stanley. *Road of Science and the Ways to God.* Chicago: University of Chicago Press, 1978.

Kass, Leon. *The Hungry Soul: Easting and the Perfection of Our Nature.* New York: Free Press, 1994.

McCarthy, John P. *Hilaire Belloc: Edwardian Radical.* Indianapolis: Liberty Press, 1978.

McNabb, Vincent. *The Catholic Church and Philosophy.* Preface by Hilaire Belloc. London: Macmillan, 1927.

O'Connor, Flannery. *Mystery and Manners.* New York: Farrar, Straus, and Giroux, 1962,

Pearce, Joseph. *Old Thunder: A Life of Hilaire Belloc.* New York: Harper/Collins, 2002.

Rousseau, Jean-Jacques. *The Reveries of the Solitary Walker.* Translated by C. Butterworth. New York: Harper Colophon, 1979.

Schall, James V. *Distinctiveness of Christianity.* San Francisco: Ignatius Press, 1982.

————, *Idylls and Rambles: Lighter Christian Essays.* San Francisco: Ignatius, 1994.

————, *Journey through Lent.* London: Catholic Truth Society, 1979.

————, *Life of the Mind: On the Joys and Travails of Thinking.* Wilmington: ISI Books, 2006.

————, *Schall on Chesterton.* Washington: The Catholic University of America Press, 2000.

Schmude, Karl. *Hilaire Belloc* Melbourne: Catholic Truth Society, 2009.

Selected Essays of G. K. Chesterton. Selected by Dorothy Collins. London: Methuen, 1951.

Speaight, Robert. *The Life of Hilaire Belloc.* New York: Farrar, Straus, & Cudahy, 1957.

_____, Editor, *Letters from Hilaire* Belloc. London: Hollis & Carter, 1958.

Weekend Wodehouse. Introduced by Hilaire Belloc. London: Pimlico Press, 1939.

Wilson, A. N. *Hilaire Belloc: A Biography.* New York: Atheneum, 1984.

Endnotes

Preface: Belloc
1   James V. Schall, *Idylls and Rambles: Shorter Christian Essays* (San Francisco: Ignatius Press, 1994).

"On the Character of Enduring Things"
1   Hilaire Belloc, *The Four Men: A Farrago* (Oxford: Oxford University Press, 1984), xix.
2   See James V. Schall, "*The Path to Rome*: Belloc's Walk a Century Later," *The Canadian C. S. Lewis Journal*, #100 (Autumn, 2001), 16–24. Chapter 6 of this book.
3   Leon Kass, *The Hungry Soul: Eating and the Perfecting of Our Nature* (New York: The Free Press, 1994).

On Endurance and Fortitude
1   Hilaire Belloc, *Selected Essays* (Harmondsworth: Penguin, 1958), 213–18.
2   *Josef Pieper—an Anthology* (San Francisco: Ignatius Press, 1989), 69–72.

At the Lake of Tiberias
1   Hilaire Belloc, *Places* (London: Cassel, 1941).

On Fame
1   Hilaire Belloc, "Truth about Modern Art," *CW*, G. K. Chesterton (San Francisco: Ignatius, 1989). XXXII, 539.

The Path to Rome: Belloc's Walk a Century Later
1   Hilaire Belloc, *The Path to Rome* (Garden City, N.Y.: Doubleday Anchor, [1902] 1956), 7.
2   *Ibid.*, 264.
3   *Ibid.*, 269.
4   *Ibid.*, 227.
5   *Ibid.*, 242.
6   *Ibid.*, 28.
7   *Ibid.*, 11.
8   *Ibid.*, 31.

9   *Ibid.*, 32.
10   *Ibid.*, 10.

Ars Taedica

1   Hilaire Belloc, *Stories, Essays, and Poems* (London: Dent, 1938).

"Islam Will Not Be the Loser"

1   Hilaire Belloc, *The Crusades* (Milwaukee: Bruce, 1937), 320–21.
2   Cited by Robin Wright, "The Chilling Goal of Islam's New Warriors," *The Los Angeles Times*, December 28, 2000.
3   Hilaire Belloc, *The Great Heresies* (New York: Sheed & Ward, MCMXXXVIII), 123. This date seems to have been September 12, but the battle took three days to be organized and completed.
4   *Ibid.*, 95–96.
5   *Ibid.*, 77–78.
6   *Ibid.*, 78. It is to be noted that the immortality of the soul and reward and punishment after death are Greek philosophical doctrines found in agreement with Christian revelation.
7   *Ibid.*, 79.
8   *Ibid.*, 81.
9   See my AIntroduction" to *G. K. Chesterton: Collected Works* (San Francisco: Ignatius Press, 2001), 25–27.
10   G. K. Chesterton, *The Everlasting Man*, in *G. K. Chesterton: Collected Works* (San Francisco: Ignatius Press, 1986), II, 360–61.
11   Stanley Jaki, *The Road of Science and the Ways to God* (Chicago: University of Chicago Press, 1978), 35–37.
12   Hilaire Belloc, *The Crusades* (Milwaukee: Bruce, 1937), 3.
13   *Ibid.,* 7–8.
14   *Ibid.*, 8.
15   *Ibid.*, 320.
16   *Ibid.*
17   Hilaire Belloc, *The Battle Ground: Syria and Palestine* (London: Lippencott, 1936), 326–27.
18   *Ibid.*, 327.

A Certain Loss

1   Albert Camus, *Lyrical and Critical Essays* (New York: Knopf, 1968).

On Thinking Continually of Those in Beatitude

1   London: Hollis & Carter, 1958.

On Towns and Places

2   Hilaire Belloc, "Home," *Selected Essays of Hilaire Belloc*, with an Introduction by J. B. Morton (London: Methuen, 1948), 53.

2   Hilaire Belloc, *The Four Men: A Farrago* (Oxford: Oxford University Press, [1911] 1984), Preface, xix.
3   Hilaire Belloc, *Places* (London: Cassell, 1942), 7.
4   *Ibid.*, 8.
5   *Ibid.*, 78.
6   *Ibid.*, 281.
7   "Stockholm Remembered," *ibid.*, 57.
8   *Ibid.*, 58.
9   *Ibid.*, 59.
10   *Ibid.*, 60.
11   *Ibid.*, 61
12   *Ibid.*, 215.
13   *Ibid.*, 216.
14   *Ibid.*, 218.
15   *Ibid.*, 219.
16   Hilaire Belloc, *Towns of Destiny* (New York: McBride, 1927), 11.
17   *Ibid.*, 75.
18   *Ibid.*, 76.
19   *Ibid.*, 77.
20   *Ibid.*, 78.
21   *Ibid.*, 79.
22   *Ibid.*, 234–35.
23   *Ibid.*, 236.
24   *Ibid.*, 237.
25   *Ibid.*, 238.

Belloc on the Metaphysics of Walking

1   Hilaire Belloc, *The Path to Rome* (Garden City, N.Y.: Doubleday Image, 1958), 114.
2   Martin Heidegger, *What Is Philosophy?* translated by J. Wilde and W. Kluback (New Haven, Ct.: College & University Press, 1956, 29.
3   Hilaire Belloc, *The Four Men: A Farrago* (Oxford: Oxford University Press, 1974), 62.
4   Hilaire Belloc, "On Old Towns," *Selected Essays of Hilaire Belloc* (London: Methuen, 1941), 277.
5   Jean-Jacques Rousseau, *The Reveries of the Solitary Walker*, trans. C. Butterworth (New York: Harper Colophon, 1979), 12.
6   Belloc, "Arles," *Hills and the Sea* (Marlboro, Vt.: The Marlboro Press, 1906), 61.
7   Belloc, "On Sailing the Seas," *Selected Essays of Hilaire Belloc, ibid.*, 143.
8   *Ibid.*, 148.
9   Belloc, "Treves," *Selected Essays*, ed. J. B. Morton (Harmondsworth: Penguin, 1958), 189–90.
10   *Ibid.*, 190–91.
11   *Ibid.*, 191.
12   Hilaire Belloc, "René Descartes," *Characters of the Reformation* (Garden City, N.Y.: Doubleday Image, 1961), 172.

13 *Ibid.*, 174.
14 *Ibid.*
15 *Ibid.*, 176.
16 *Ibid.*
17 Belloc, "Blaise Pascal," *ibid.*, 178.
18 *Ibid.*, 181.
19 *Ibid.*, 182.
20 *Ibid.*, 183.
21 Belloc, ALynn," *Hills and the Sea*, ibid. 100.
22 *Ibid.*, 100–101.
23 *Ibid.*, 104.

"In the Presence of So Wonderful a Thing"
1   London: Methuen, 1941.

The Charm of Belloc: "On Caring Too Much"
1   Hilaire Belloc, "Jane Austen," *Selected Essays* (Harmondsworth: Penguin, 1958), 196–97. (Originally found in *The Silence of the Sea.*)
2   Hilaire Belloc, *The Four Men* (London: Thomas Nelson, 1912), 95.
3   *Ibid.*, 3.
4   *Ibid.*, viii.
5   Hilaire Belloc, "Lynn," *Hills and the Sea* (Marlboro, VT.: The Marlboro Press, 1906), 104.
6   Hilaire Belloc, *The Path to Rome* (Garden City, N.Y.: Doubleday Image, 1958), 196.
7   *Ibid.*, 49–50.
8   James V. Schall, "The Last Medieval Monarchy: Chesterton and Belloc on the Philosophic Import of the American Experience," *Faith & Reason*, XIV (Summer 1988), 167–88. Belloc wrote a book on America entitled *The Contrast* (London: J. W. Arrowsmith, 1923).
9   George and Weedon Grossmith, *The Diary of a Nobody* (London: The Folio Society, [1892] 1969), 11, 162–63.
10 Robert Speaight, *Letters from Hilaire Belloc* (London: Hollis & Carter, 1958).
11 Maurice Baring, *Lost Lectures, or the Fruits of Experience* (New York: A. A. Knopf, 1932).
12 Hilaire Belloc, "The Death of the Wandering Peter," *Selected Essays, ibid.*, 75.
13 Hilaire Belloc, *Danton: A Study* (London: Thomas Nelson, [1899] 1928) 335–36.
14 *Path to Rome, ibid.*, 270.
15 James V. Schall, "On Leaving Rome," *The Distinctiveness of Christianity* (San Francisco: Ignatius Press, 1982). 13–33.
16 *Ibid.*, 102.

Harbor in the North
1   Belloc, "The Harbour of the North," *Hills and the Sea, ibid.*, 216.

2   Ibid., 217.
3   Ibid., 218–19.

Conclusion

1   Flannery O'Connor, Mystery and Manners (New York: Farrar, Straus, and Giroux, 1962).

Index

Cubism, 21
Cuppy, Will, 95

Danton, 1, 140–142
Delphi, 108
democracy, 57–58, 96
Descartes, 113–115
devil, 11–12, 23, 114, 137, 139–140, 144
Dickens, 75, 128
doctrine, 8–9, 19, 22–23, 54–55, 58, 65–67, 82, 86–87, 92, 115
dogma, 65, 86, 138
Downs, 8, 12, 14

Eliot, T.S., 10
Elodie (Belloc), 2, 64, 118, 135
endurance, 16–17
England, 3, 7, 31, 38, 41, 56, 69, 71–73, 79, 84, 94, 108, 116, 126–129, 135
Erasmus, 73
Eros, 111
Europe, xii, 3, 5, 8, 17, 29–30, 32–33, 54, 56, 58, 70, 77–78, 80–81, 85–86, 89, 112–115, 135, 153–154, 156, 163–164
The Everlasting Man, 55
evil, 17, 36, 54, 83–84, 89, 92–93, 134, 142, 146

faith, xi,1, 3, 9, 32–33, 64, 66–67, 69, 83, 113, 115, 139, 142, 153–154
fame, 19, 21–23, 128

The Four Men, 2–3, 7–8, 10–14, 32, 78–80, 105–106, 134, 144, 162
fortitude, 15–17
freedom, 35, 52, 79, 109, 144, 159, 162
friendship, 64, 67, 83, 87, 92, 146
futurism, 21

Garden of Eden, 9, 31
Germany, 83, 100, 112
GK's Weekly, 94
Great Heresies, 1, 18

Hastings, 39
Hattin, 18–19, 56
Haut Brion, 64, 67
Hell, 9, 13, 120–122
Hills and the Sea, 1, 72, 118, 120, 156
history, xii, 1, 3–4, 9, 18–19, 36–38, 57, 60, 63, 81, 89, 92, 94, 96, 103, 109–110, 117, 123–126, 135, 163–164
"Home," 77, 131
home, 7–10, 14, 26, 30, 68, 77–78, 86, 134, 136, 140, 142, 151, 162–163
Homer, 39, 133–134
Horace, 42

Idylls & Rambles, 3, 25
immortality, 2, 22–23, 54, 66, 68, 71, 86, 105, 128, 139, 165
inns, 8, 11–13, 32, 90, 105–106, 111, 117, 134, 144, 164